DEDICATION

To Phil, who made this possible

ACKNOWLEDGMENTS

Thanks go first to God for his healing in our lives personally through Jesus and the Holy Spirit. We can only give from what we've first received. Thank you, Father!

This was never a solo. My deepest thanks go to all of those who made this possible. But three people deserve very special recognition.

...*Dixon Kinser,* who believed in this enough to allow us to use his group as guinea pigs for each new topic, to go through the process himself and be changed, and to be our constant encourager.

...*Kristin Kinser,* for her dedication, creative ideas, writing and rewriting, work and re-work, edit and reedit, and for keeping all the details together. Kristin, your name belongs on the cover—and it is, in my eyes.

...*My husband, Phil,* for his vision and perseverance, editing, collecting, structuring, and organizing my random thoughts—and the tenacity to see this through to the end. Phil, you also belong on the cover. This is yours and Kristin's more than mine.

Many thanks to the original cross\fire team whose brainstorming led to the program: Cathy Morrill, Phil Coy, and Baxter Peffer. And thanks to Matt Fairfield, Kelly Sullivan, and Kim Milanovich, whose additions focused the material. (The "rocks" interaction on forgiveness is courtesy of Shery Shaw.)

Finally, thanks to the kids from St. David's youth group who were so willing to deal with their own stuff and allow God to heal them. We learned as we taught and were amazed.

—*Wendy Coy*

Tough Stuff: 12 Comprehensive Sessions on Growing Through Life's Deepest Pains

Copyright © 2003 innerACTS

innerACTS, PO Box 179, Ambridge, Pennsylvania 15003

Youth Specialties Books, 300 South Pierce Street, El Cajon, California 92020, are published by Zondervan, 5300 Patterson Avenue Southeast, Grand Rapids, Michigan 49530.

Library of Congress Cataloging-in-Publication Data

Coy, Wendy, 1954-
   Tough Stuff: 12 comprehensive sessions on growing through life's deepest
   pains / by Wendy Coy.
      p. cm.
   Includes bibliographical references.
   ISBN 0-310-24550-8 (pbk.)
   1. Church group work with teenagers. 2. Adjustment (Psychology)—Religious aspects—
   Christianity—Study and teaching. I. Title.
BV4447 .c65 2003
268'.433—dc21

2002012242

Web site addresses listed in this book were current at the time of publication. Please contact Youth Specialties via e-mail (YS@YouthSpecialties.com) to report URLs that are no longer operational and replacement URLs if available.

Edited by Dave Urbanski
Cover and interior design by Left Coast
Production assistance by Nicole Davis

Printed in the United States of America

04 05 06 07 08 09 / VG / 10 9 8 7 6 5 4

TABLE OF CONTENTS

Abuse, porn, homosexuality, broken families, hiding, shame, addiction, masks, idolatry, promiscuity. Do you have students in your group who are struggling to follow Jesus but are stuck in their growth? Have you hit the realities of horrendous family situations, painful relationships, or senseless acting out? Do you have leaders with obvious gifting but also with similar issues that threaten to sidetrack them from God's plans?

You see the problems. You want to help. What can you do? Can you help students in pain? Can you help the ones who're headed for real trouble?

Tough Stuff was created to give you the content and methods to address the toughest issues head on. For too long, our only answers have been "read your Bible and pray" or "let's get you into counseling." For too many students, it's not working. They can't or won't go to counseling. Their problems seem insurmountable and unsolvable. Trite answers don't cut it. Students want to know whether this God stuff works!

Students today believe if God can't meet them in the midst of their pain, then he's not big enough or real enough to be worth it. But Jesus will meet kids in their deepest places of pain! He is able to heal even the worst damage done by a broken world.

Tough Stuff is not for the faint of heart. It will cost you.

It will cost you more prep time than you've probably ever imagined before. It will challenge you to teach with new content—with new eyes. It will demand that you drop any "talking head" teaching and get real with tough topics and with kids. It will put you into the hot seat to address issues that you want to ignore or sweep under the rug. It will get you in trouble with parents trying to maintain myths of perfect families and perfect children. It will challenge you to pray for specific healing in students and in yourselves. It will destroy your I-have-it-all-together image (your pride?) as you share your own struggles with the tough issues of your past. It will put you squarely in the sights of the enemy—you can expect direct spiritual attacks.

Yes, it will cost you. But it will be worth it.

Students' lives will be radically changed! They will understand more about the depth of God's love for them and God's ability to wash away pain and cleanse their sin. They will understand more about themselves and how and why they respond the way they do. Students who struggle with deep, life-dominating sin patterns will begin to experience freedom. The ones heading for trouble will find God to be more real than their pain. That's transforming power!

Jesus said that those who've been forgiven much will love much (Luke 7:47). Touch students' deepest pains with the healing of their hearts, and you'll have kids who know that God is real and are sold out to him.

There's nothing new here. It's all in the Book. Healing is about the reality of living in grace, confessing our sins, receiving forgiveness, forgiving others, renouncing our idols, and living in the love of God. This is "mere Christianity"—unleashing the power of God to transform our hearts by being gut-level honest with God, with ourselves, and with each other. And expecting that God will be gut-level real with us!

The material that's included in *Tough Stuff* has been used for more than five years in high school youth groups, on college retreats, for seminars and conferences. It's been taught in seminary-level courses and run with junior highers on weekends. It's been tested and tailored and tweaked. But there's room for you to put your own spin on it to make it work for you. And the FAQ section, as well as the many sidebars within, will help guide you as you tackle these topics. Hang on tight!

Tough Stuff is for high school and college students. Junior high students can handle some topics, but they aren't developmentally ready for others. The FAQs include suggestions on how to approach different age groups and maturity levels. Healing is tough stuff. The issues are complex. The pain is intense. Students' faith is on the line. Don't assume you can just pick up a lesson from this book and "wing it" without prep. The most effective way to communicate truth is to interact with it. That means teaching by simply standing up and talking is definitely "out"—and activity is in. Dramas, improvs, skits, hands-on activities, video clips, music, and handouts are a beginning to prompt your thinking so you can communicate truth in as many different ways possible. But they all need preparation. There are materials, props, and "stuff" that you need to gather in advance. And there are roles to play in sketches that you may want to prep in advance with your leadership team.

Tough Stuff is intended as the content of your group meetings. Use one or all of the topics, depending upon what you need at the time. One topic will work for a meeting of about one hour in length—there are time estimates for each of the "interactions" in each chapter. You can extend the discussion times and even spread the topic over several meetings if you'd like. You can add to our suggestions for music or video clips. You can invent more improv sketches. What you do and what you add depends on how far and deep you want to go. The topics work best in the sequence presented, but you can pick and choose their order as it fits your group. But it's best to start with the chapter on "Denial" (chapter one) since it offers a strong introduction to the healing process.

We've found the most effective environment for healing involves four key elements. We encourage you to include each of these for your group as you go through *Tough Stuff*.

1. **WORSHIP.** This unlocks a door for God to come in and begin his work in our hearts. In worship we open ourselves to God's interaction as we declare his power and love. In worship we look beyond ourselves and our pain and focus instead on Jesus. With all our understanding and our psychology, it's God who is the healer. Worship softens our hearts and allows God to do his surgery.

2. **INTERACTIVE TEACHING.** Tackling difficult topics requires that you communicate clearly and present the topic in ways that kids can grasp and apply. We use a variety of methods to communicate the key truths about God and ourselves. Instead of "talking at" kids, we believe in inductive methods, allowing kids to come to their own conclusions. The core content for each topic and the methods to address them are the bulk of the material in *Tough Stuff*. But the style and the way you present the picture or concept is totally up to you!

3. **SMALL GROUPS.** Kids are talking with each other all the time. Small groups allow them to share in a safe environment. *Tough Stuff* has small group questions for each topic, which allow honesty and vulnerability in "bounded" small groups. In order to make it safer to share and keep it appropriate, we recommend that you set up same-sex and same-age small groups. There are some guidelines for small groups in the FAQ section that may be helpful to you. You can use *Tough Stuff* without small groups, but students really benefit from sharing their own stories together.

4. **HEALING PRAYER.** Prayer unleashes the power of God to actually change our hearts. Prayer is the essential ingredient. Pray for your kids in the large group, show students how to pray for each other in small groups, get adults to intercede for your youth during your meeting times, find people who know how to pray for healing. It doesn't matter what the model is. It may be charismatic, evangelical, liturgical, small-group oriented, missions-minded, Protestant, Catholic, Orthodox, or any other denominational framework. What's important is that you invite God into the healing process and encourage young people to open themselves up to God's touch and his power.

There's nothing new about this model. It's from Acts 2:42: "They devoted themselves to the apostles' teaching and to the fellowship, to the breaking of bread and to prayer." Worship, teaching, small groups, and prayer—powerful tools that God will use to bring healing to his people.

We pray God's blessing on you as you dive into *Tough Stuff*!

—*Wendy Coy*

What's in the *Tough Stuff* curriculum?

Each chapter covers a single topic of Tough Stuff. A cover page will give you a quick reference to the key concepts. You can quickly scan what's in the chapter as you decide what's appropriate for your group. Also included are the interactions for presenting the topic. Each interaction is a stand-alone segment that has a specific point or two to make. You can take a single interaction for an entire meeting if you want to really dive deep.

Each interaction has a brief summary, the time required, a list of the materials needed, and the preparation that's needed. Be aware that some preparation may take more planning than just pulling stuff together 10 minutes before your meeting!

Each interaction is completely scripted out. In the scripting, the main teaching points that you should emphasize are highlighted. *Tough Stuff* uses an inductive teaching style with lots of open-ended questions to get students thinking and reacting. (And don't worry—the desired responses from your group are also included so you have some idea where the conversation ought to go.)

Kids want to tell their stories and to hear the stories of others who've struggled with tough issues in similar ways. You'll be prompted at certain points to share a personal testimony on a particular topic. Examples of testimonies from the original team that developed *Tough Stuff* are included so you have a sense of the style of personal sharing that's been effective. If your testimony doesn't apply, find another leader who can share an appropriate story from his or her life. You'll be amazed at how may stories you really do have!

Where clips from videos are referred, the start and stop times and some intro and exit lines are included so that you can cue the video up in advance to the right spot and know when to end. When this was first developed, the original team rented or bought the videos and used two VCRs to copy the clips so that it would flow more smoothly—so these times are approximate! (Definitely an amateur job but it didn't cost anything, either.) Or maybe you have someone who's into video editing to do a more polished job. Please, however, respect the copyright laws.

Finally, each chapter includes discussion questions for your small groups and a list of biblical references related to the topic. There's also a short annotated bibliography of resources for additional study if you feel the need to delve more deeply into a particular topic.

Basic Equipment You Need…
- Bibles
- Paper for notes
- Pens or crayons.

At times the curriculum will refer to writing on a whiteboard. That can mean a real whiteboard, a chalkboard, transparency and overheads, posterboard, blank newsprint, or anything large enough so the whole group can read it. There are lots of suggestions for video clips, so a VCR and large-screen TV or projector is really helpful, too. A boom box works fine for music tracks if you don't have a sound system.

The following are frequently asked questions from youth workers who want to begin to open up these topics in the context of their youth groups.

It's easier to just refer my "problem kids" to counseling.
Why should I subject my whole group to this stuff?
Because your kids are already talking about this stuff together. Do you want to be in on the conversation or not? The topics are unfortunately all too common in students' lives. If one young person is in crisis, then others may be dealing with less extreme variations of the same thing—and also want help. We believe that healing is best handled in community rather than in isolation. Yes, it's hard. Yes, it's risky. But the rewards definitely outweigh the risk. Still, do your homework first and be prepared to deal with kids' real pain as you go through *Tough Stuff*.

How do I deal with topics that are awkward for the group to talk about?
One reason that students may find it difficult to talk about a topic is because the topic itself may feel shameful, as though it shouldn't even be mentioned. That's where you come in. As the authority, you will set the tone for what can be talked about, what is talked about seriously, and what is taken as a joke or too lightly. First, you need to deal with any shame issues surrounding a topic that you have personally. If you're embarrassed, your group will sense it in a heartbeat. Second, you need to communicate clearly that its okay to talk about the "taboo" topics, and that you'll give the subject a fair, objective, and serious hearing. Third, you need to be sensitive to the emotional maturity of your group concerning particular topics. Some topics may not be appropriate for where the group is right now.

I have kids from family situations that are pretty unhealthy.
How do I deal with that?
The more unhealthy the family situation, the more desperate those kids are to talk about it with someone who can help give them perspective and hope. You need to help them along to understand what's going on at home. And you need to do this being very careful to not bash parents in the process. Everyone sins and is sinned against; we're all broken. Be careful that you don't place blame on parents. For students in difficult family situations, the answer is boundaries, boundaries, and more boundaries. Teach the Boundaries topic, suggest they read *Boundaries* by Cloud and Townsend, start a separate group for those with the most difficult circumstances so they're able to share more fully and really work out solutions. Help them set healthy boundaries that respect their parents' rightful authority without compromising their identities as their own, separate persons. You might want to recommend an adult education class on *Boundaries* in order to introduce the topic to adults in your church.

What do I do if parents aren't supportive but a student really wants help with an issue?

We've heard the "but my family is fine" line lots of times. Many parents are less willing to admit there are problems than their children are to deal with them. When we run a series on healing, we start by letting parents know what topics we'll be covering and set expectations about how they are treated. An information night for the parents may be a terrific opportunity to start some communication. We also get parental permission. If a parent says "No," then we must respect their authority.

How do I address issues that I fear parents might not want brought up?

Be aware of the cultural and social contexts of your students' families and what they're already dealing with. A parents' night for discussing in advance the topics may be a great opportunity to get an idea of what's acceptable and what's not. Take on the topics that you can and drop the rest. We deal with gender and sexual orientation in *Tough Stuff*—and that's on purpose. We really believe that Christian kids need to have a Christian perspective on sexuality and homosexuality. To skip the topic just because it's controversial doesn't prepare kids for the battleground of life. So dive in—but sensitively.

Is there a sequence to the sessions or can I just pick and choose?

The topics are in the order that we recommend, but you may pick and choose as you see fit. We recommend you use the Denial topic as your initial session so you can introduce the whole concept of healing and allow kids to begin looking at issues. We cover the Parents topic early in the series in order to free students to receive from God as he is rather than staying distant from him because of faulty filters from their family.

Some of my younger students giggle and get embarrassed with any mention about sex or sexuality. How do I address that?

Some of these topics aren't appropriate for junior highers—or even for teenagers who aren't emotionally ready. Watch that your own, personal embarrassment doesn't infect the group. If you deal with the topics seriously, so will your group. Also try to not use the current slang for sexual functions. For example, if you use the word *masturbation* instead of any number of current vernacular expressions, you're much more likely to be taken seriously.

Some words seem not to be acceptable in any context. Any advice?

Be sensitive to your context and what parents will think appropriate. We encourage students to use proper terms, not slang, but to go ahead and talk about the real issues openly and frankly. (Your students are talking about them already anyway!)

What about junior highers? How do they deal with tough stuff?

Some topics aren't going to work with junior highers. A lot of junior high students still want to see their parents as heroes and their families as perfect. Topics that have worked well with junior highers are Masks, Idols, Identity, and Forgiveness. With junior highers, be more directive than open-ended in discussing topics. For high schoolers, it's better to let kids struggle to understand; just draw out answers from them and allow them come to their own conclusions.

I don't know all that much about some of these topics. How much do I have to know before I teach the curriculum?

Not all that much more than the most knowledgeable kid. Do some reading; we've made recommendations. Get to a conference on healing. The best way by far is to start looking at your own issues. We all have issues, and dealing with our own "stuff" gives us more ability and authority to minister to others.

I sense that kids are talking a lot about these issues but don't seem to be willing to share in our small groups. How do I get them to open up in the groups?

First, be sure that you as a leader are modeling the kind of honesty and vulnerability you desire from your students. They won't go one inch further than you. Second, small groups need to be safe. Here are some guidelines to help:

- Respect confidentiality—except in cases where there's intent to harm oneself or others or another's property.
- Encourage honesty. Teach the Masks topic.
- Don't allow advice giving, "bible bullets," and quick-fix answers (e.g., "If you just…"). These are a sure way to shut down someone sharing an area of real struggle. The answers are never "Just read your Bible more and pray more!"

How important is it that I share my own story?

Very. Your story opens up your students to tell theirs and to talk about real issues. It allows them to know that you've been in the same place that some of them are now. Here are a couple of guidelines about sharing your own "stuff." First, share issues that you've had some measure of success with. It's never appropriate to share something that's an ongoing struggle or that's "in your face" right now. Second, be sure that your sharing benefits your group and not your own needs. That's NEVER appropriate. A testimony should allow students to identify with you and also to have hope for change.

What if I don't have small groups?

We strongly believe in small groups as a way to encourage sharing, but they aren't essential. It's just a lot easier with small groups.

How can I get more help?

Check out the recommended readings. If you have students dealing with homosexuality, *The Map* from Exodus International is an excellent interactive CD for a young person to individually explore the topic from a Christian healing perspective. *SOULutions* from innerACTS is a good student workbook for individual study. (innerACTS and other groups are available to come in to train you or lead retreats on these topics. See page 159 for details.)

I deal with some of these issues myself and am still "in process." How far along in my own healing do I have to be in order to begin to help my students with the same issues?

If you wait until you're "done," you may never start. Just be sure you're prepared if you teach a topic that may still be a struggle for you. If you're concerned, get someone else who has overcome that area to come and teach for you. Just be sure that you aren't sharing too much of your current struggle and too little of your victories over it.

What do I do if a student is talking about suicide?

When you open up tough topics and give students a safe place to share, you'll get honest, very real, and sometimes very scary feelings. Some students may talk about suicidal feelings, wanting to hurt themselves—some may have cut themselves already. But it's important to distinguish between random thoughts and feelings and planned intent. Remember that you as a youth worker have a legal responsibility called "mandated reporting" whereby you must report child abuse, sexual abuse, or suicide to the authorities. Laws vary by state, so please find out what your requirements are. Talk with your pastor about how to handle these situations in advance. Have that talk today! It's a lot easier to come up with a strategy in advance than to have a suicidal teenager on your hands and need to deal in the emotional turmoil of the moment.

(A special note about cutting, since it's become quite common: Cutting isn't necessarily related to suicide at all, although it still must be taken very seriously. Inflicting physical pain can provide a focus and actually relieve a student's intense emotional pain. This behavior can become addictive—for some students, it's better to hurt on the outside than on the inside. You need to encourage student who are cutting regularly to get more help than you can provide.)

My kids don't seem to have any hesitations about talking about anything at all—even in mixed groups. Is that okay?

One consequence of the overwhelming amount of sexually explicit and sexually suggestive material bombarding young people is that there seems to be no room anymore for reticence about some topics. For a great book that may challenge some of your students, especially girls, we recommend *A Return to Modesty* by Wendy Shalit (Simon and Schuster, 1999). Although not a Christian, Shalit describes really well the current pressures facing young women, including sleeping around, eating disorders, and body image. Her conclusion is that the "lost virtue" of modesty is what's called for. So when we run groups with this material, we insist on same-sex small groups. This allows more freedom for guys to share with other guys and girls to share with other girls without things getting too embarrassing or sexually charged. In this wide-open, free-for-all society, there are still topics that are best left undiscussed in mixed groups. While we don't recommend you squelch discussion, you might want to gently nudge kids to not talk about some topics in mixed settings. Some topics—even when discussed in a same-sex group setting—will spawn unhealthy mental images or trigger fantasy. Guys are particularly prone toward this.

**Small groups are great, but my group doesn't pray out loud.
How important is prayer?**

There are lots of ways to pray, out loud or silently, with the Scriptures, with laying on hands, using sacramental oil and water. Regardless of your group's "style," prayer for healing unlocks the power of God to touch and heal hurting people. Psychological understanding may be helpful to provide perspective on what's going on, but God changes hearts. So pray hard, get intercessors to pray for your group during meeting times, and encourage kids to pray for one another in small groups. Above all, be the model yourself of how you want your students to pray.

**I don't know anything about prayer for healing.
Where can I get more information?**

We recommend several of the books by Leanne Payne, especially Restoring the Christian Soul through Healing Prayer. But reading a book isn't the most effective way to learn about healing prayer. Receiving prayer is the absolute best way to learn about it! Find someone who's good at it and get prayer yourself! Then try out what works for you and your group.

Some of these activities seem like a lot of work to set up. Is it worth it?

We tried the "talking head" approach to teaching these topics. And while the topics themselves get interest, it's really easy for kids to just tune out. What we've discovered is that students need to experience truth, not just know about it. That's led us to develop as close to a purely interactive and inductive teaching program as possible. You'll see, for example, that we slip a lot of the content of the topic into the wrap-ups after the interaction gives that "teachable moment" —that really helps illustrate an issue. If you grab the group with the material and leave a visual picture of the point, they'll remember it for years. (We come across kids who four years later can relate the "tree" diagram from the Denial chapter and talk about what it means to them. Do you remember the Sunday sermon last week?) Yeah, it's a lot of work—but it's definitely worth it.

Some of this seems juvenile. Does this really work?

That's up to you in how you set it up. If you think it's juvenile then that's what your group will think. We've found that encouraging students to see the outward action as representative of an inward attitude or movement of God is very helpful. That's what a sacrament is anyway. Smashing a plaster of Paris idol can either be a funny exercise or a life-changing decision to renounce an idol in our hearts. You set the tone. Kids will want to deal with God on these issues in a serious way. If you let them, they will.

Do I need to have adults in small groups or can my student leaders handle it?

That's up to you. If you have an adult in a small group, the kids will let him or her take the lead and will only share to the level of honesty of the adult leader. You may want to coach your adult leaders on what's appropriate and what's not. We also believe that mature Christian teenagers are perfectly able to lead small groups. If you want to go this route, gather your small group leaders into a separate team and provide some training and guidance—perhaps even go through the curriculum with them first! Be sure that you follow up with them afterward and coach them on situations where they felt awkward or uncomfortable. It's an ideal leadership training ground.

What's the most effective setting for this curriculum?

The ideal setting is a voluntary group of discipleship-level kids. Not all your kids need this stuff, and not all are ready even if they need it. But for those who are, this can absolutely revolutionize their spiritual lives and prepare them to minister to others. In our setting, we wrap worship, interactive teaching, small groups, and healing prayer together.

My whole group isn't ready for this, but I have some kids who really need it. What can I do?

Run *Tough Stuff* for a select group of kids who are ready for it and want it. Or if you aren't sure your group is ready, use a couple of topics on a weekend retreat and see how it goes. We've designed this to be a group experience, not one-on-one work. If you have only one or two individuals who want something, check out "SOULutions," a student workbook from innerACTS. It addresses many of these topics and provides thought questions for follow-up and directions for prayer. It's very useful for individual discipleship.

1 "REALLY, I'M FINE"

ESCAPING DENIAL AND ADMITTING OUR PAIN

MAIN POINTS:

1. We're often in denial about the pain in our lives.

2. When we sin, we go against God's plan for our lives.

3. It's often impossible to control our sin because it's rooted in the past.

   - In the face of God's perfection, we are ashamed of our sin and hurts.

   - Beneath the sin and hurts, we have legitimate and God-given needs.

   - We're also ashamed of our needs and see them as the problem.

   - We respond by hating ourselves and/or hating others.

4. Jesus wants to forgive our sins, heal our hearts, and fill our needs.

   - Jesus isn't ashamed of us or angry with us. Jesus loves us.

   - When we confess our sins and forgive those who've hurt us, we're able to receive healing from Jesus and allow him to meet our needs.

LESSON SEGMENTS:

The Black Knight
Tree-Roots Interaction
Tree Diagram

IN THIS LESSON...

Moving from denial to understanding...

Getting rid of shame and self-hatred...

Dealing with the roots of our sin...

Finding Jesus' healing for our lives...

16

"THE BLACK KNIGHT"

THE POINT: We deny our obvious wounds all the time by saying "I'm fine."

TIME NEEDED: 5 Minutes

MATERIALS: Video of *Monty Python and the Holy Grail*
Large screen TV or video projector

PREPARATION: Cue video to the Black Knight scene
Start: 13:05 (the Black Knight fighting another knight)

STOP: 17:24 (Arthur rides off)

Stage: Play "Black Knight" scene.

What did you think about the Black Knight's state of mind?
Desired response: Help group to see the ludicrous denial involved in the Black Knight's insistence that he is still able to fight.

He's really a sad case. The Black Knight is gradually reduced to nothing but a torso, and still he thinks it's only a flesh wound! He has a problem. No arms, no legs—but he thinks he can go on fighting.

We laugh, but we do this all the time in our emotional lives. We run around with all sorts of wounds, emotionally broken and torn, and we pretend everything's okay: "I'm fine," we say. We have pain stuffed deep inside, but we say, "I'm fine."

Despite his denial, the Black Knight must have been in pain—after all, King Arthur chopped off his limbs in a fight! Despite our denials, we have pain, too. There's a reason for our pain. We usually don't have a chance to look at that. There's always room to say "stop doing what's wrong," but usually not very many chances to look at why we're in pain. In this session we'll be looking at the roots of the pain in our lives.

TREE-ROOTS INTERACTION

THE POINT: Some sins we struggle with over and over again but can't seem to control. These tough sins in our lives have roots of commission (things that hurt us) or roots of omission (things that weren't done but should have been). And then shame covers all—the sin, the hurts, and the underlying needs.

SUMMARY: Students build a "tree" that traces the roots of sin in their lives—from our unmet needs (underground and invisible, like the roots) to outward, sinful behaviors, actions, or attitudes (leaves and branches).

TIME NEEDED: 35 minutes

MATERIALS: White bed sheet with "Shame" written on it with large black letters
Markers
Orange and yellow paper leaves (make enough for each student to have 4 to 5)
10 to 12 sheets of green construction paper (for "grass"—i.e., obvious, visible, surface causes for our behaviors)
10 to 12 sheets of brown construction paper (for "roots"—deep, invisible, forgotten causes of our behavior)
2 sheets of yellow construction paper, one labeled "Self-Hatred," the other "Hatred of others"
2 large hearts made of red construction paper—one cut in two, the other whole
Several rolls of double-sided tape (to attach leaves to the trees)
Large wooden cross—approximately five feet high.

ROLES NEEDED: Teacher/narrator
Assistant to teacher/narrator (hands labels and materials to teacher, helps with props)
Jesus (needs to be prepped before meeting)
Tree(s)—1 or 2 volunteers

PREPARATION: Cut out the leaves and the two hearts before the meeting.
Have markers and tape ready.
Have prepared labels for some of the deeper issues (grass level and deeper roots).

ROLE PREP: No preparation is needed for the person playing the Tree.
The person playing the role of Jesus needs to be coached in advance.

INTRODUCTION:

In our lives, there are roots to our pain—and yet we often pretend that everything's okay. We're going to take a few minutes to look at these using a picture.

Take a deep breath—and think of yourself as a tree.

During the fall, trees in the temperate parts of the world are full of orange and yellow leaves and scarlet leaves. They're bright, they're conspicuous, they're impossible to hide—just like some of the sin in our lives.

Let's look at the leaves as what we think, do, or feel. We all have both good and bad leaves in our lives. But it usually seems that the bad leaves are more visible. Stuff we do, attitudes, sin, junk we'd rather hide. It's the stuff we don't like, the stuff we're ashamed of.

Okay, enough with talking about trees. I need someone here to "be" a tree for the next 30 minutes—a brave, strong volunteer to stand up here to be a tree for a while...

Stage: Have a volunteer come up and stand like a tree.
You can use 2 volunteers if you have a large group.

CONTENT:

Let's look at the leaves here as representing all the unhealthy things in our lives—the things we usually try to hide or get rid of... the things that separate us from Jesus.

The leaves are your job: you get to name the leaves—that is, the unhealthy things-and plaster them on our tree here. Can anyone give me some examples?

Desired Response: Ask the group to call out unhealthy things. Tell the group that these are not your own personal issues, but just things you've seen or know of. Prompt specifics such as addictions, violence, pornography, perpetrating abuse, et cetera.

It can be little stuff like being addicted to chocolate or big stuff like sex before marriage—and everything in between. Okay, now we're going to write down these things on some leaves and plaster the tree.

Stage: Ask participants to get into groups of 3 and brainstorm lots of unhealthy things. Participants should write one issue on each leaf. Then have kids come up and tape the leaves on the tree. Take only 3 minutes or so at this. Typical leaves:

Abuse, Getting drunk or high, Alcohol abuse, Addiction, Gossip, Greed, Hatred, Pornography, Judging others, Inappropriate anger, Lying, Bad language, Covetousness, Lust, Stealing, Pride, Selfishness, Fighting with family, Laziness

Look at what we've got here.

Call out the unhealthy behaviors as they're pinned on the tree. Note that some of the time, we just make bad choices and choose to do the wrong things. Or get trapped in a situation and do the wrong thing and

LEADER'S NOTES:

To get kids actually thinking and talking about the issues they wrestle with, your students must believe that you'll really deal authentically with those issues. You may want to demonstrate your openness by encouraging kids to specifically name struggles or unhealthy behavior that aren't typically mentioned in church or youth group settings. If your group is less mature, you may have some kids get embarrassed or start giggling. In such cases you can keep the discussion constructive by using proper terminology rather than the locker room versions. Furthermore, if your kids can handle it, hint at or suggest outright some issues you feel ought to be named publicly—or have some leaves already labeled with those things.

don't realize it until later. Some students will note things that someone else did to them (e.g., being abused) as sins. Take the opportunity to remind the students that our sins are our responses, attitudes, and actions—not what someone else has done to us. What's been done to us is someone else's sin (e.g., having been abused in not your sin, but being the abuser definitely is).

Stage: Ask the following question to the "tree person."

How do you feel with all this stuff all over you?
Desired Response: Dirty, yucky, ashamed.

> **POINT:** When we really see our sin, we often respond with shame about who we are and what we've done.

The first thing we feel is ashamed...

Stage: Put the "Shame" sheet over the tree.

What's shame?
Desired Response: Shame is about who we are, not just about what we've done.

Shame is feeling bad about who we are, not just about what we've done. (Not a technical definition, but it works.)

Once shame gets in the picture, there's not much else you can do. Everything gets worse. Everything is covered up. We think shame hides us, even protects us from the world. In reality, others can see us—and our shame—but we're the ones who suffer because shame cuts us off from other people and from God. Shame is the first thing we must deal with.

Stage: Pull the "Shame" sheet back a bit so you can still work with tree (and so the volunteer can breathe!)

Now let's talk about the heart of this tree. In a human being, the heart is the home of our emotions, our self-image, our conscience. If you were this tree, would your heart be happy? How would your heart feel if this was your tree?
Desired Response: Unhappy, sad.

Okay, let's put a broken heart on the tree.

Stage: Tape two pieces of a broken heart on the tree.

Is this all there is to the tree? What other parts of a tree are there?
Desired Response: Trunk and roots

Every plant grows in soil. How might the environment—the soil, the water, the weather—affect the tree?
Desired Response: Good soil allows growth, bad soil doesn't, etc.

And how about the roots? All trees have roots. There are roots at ground level, weaving through the grass. Let's say these surface roots are the things that happen to us...things that were done to us...or things that weren't done that should

ONE MAY BE PREDISPOSED TO...	IF ONE HAS EXPERIENCED...
(Leaves)	(Grass level roots)
Violence	Physical abuse Abuse in the family Witnessed violence early on

Pornography	Saw pornography early –
	    Which breaks boundaries and
	    awakens sexual desire too early,
	    Breaks innocence of childhood
	Sexual abuse

Alcoholism	Alcoholism in the family
	    Alcohol used as an escape,
	    reward or bribe

Insecurity	Abandonment or neglect
Anger	Abuse either physical or sexual Abandonment
Emotional dependencies	Lack of attachment in early years
Isolation	Neglect
Promiscuity	Sexual abuse
Fear of men	Abuse by male Abusive father
Hatred of women	Abuse by woman Domineering mother
Poor self-image	Abuse – feeling that "I deserved it"
Eating disorders	Extremely controlling parents Image-driven family
Perfectionism	Legalistic, demanding parents
Controlling	Chaos in home
Fear	Abuse, threatening parents

LEADER'S NOTES:

Emphasize that being abused is not a sin. Being abusive is. One of the most common things an abuser tells a victim is, "It's your fault." We need to be quick to correct any attempt to "confess" abuse as a person's own sin. While we're not responsible for being abused, we are responsible for our response.

Not all of our behavior or every sin has a deep, dark past that needs to be investigated. We all have sins we commit that we can simply confess and receive forgiveness for (1 John 1:9). They don't seem to come up as repeated patterns. But we also have sins that we've committed over and over again, that we've confessed time after time, and that we can't just seem to get beyond. It's these "stuck places" that bear looking at more closely to see if there are roots to it. The act of beginning to uncover the roots to why we act in certain ways often leads to understanding and helps us get beyond being dominated by our sins.

Telling your own story in your own words is incredibly helpful. Kids need models for how to overcome personal struggles. Your personal vulnerability will set the tone for the level of honesty that kids are comfortable sharing. They won't share any more honestly than you will.

What kind of personal struggles are appropriate for you to share? The one with which you've had some measure of healing. Issues of yours that are unresolved or currently painful won't communicate the hope for healing that kids need to hear. Remember, you need to have resources to address your own issues in settings other than with kids you're leading! You're there to minister to them and NEVER to get your own needs met through them.

This testimony and the other testimony examples in this book are actual stories from the team of youth workers who created this program. We found that these kinds of testimonies effectively illustrate the point with kids. Still, although they are actual situations in the lives of actual people, your own testimony will be far more personal and far more effective.

If you don't have a testimony or story that applies, find another leader (student or adult) who can share a story.

have been. These ground-level roots have an effect on the leaves and the branches. Let's take a look at some of the leaves and see what kind of roots might have produced those leaves... and made those leaves so hard to die.

Let's take violence, for example. What are some of its roots? It just doesn't happen: something causes us to act violently.

Stage: Choose some leaves that are relatively easy to trace back to past circumstances. For example, violence—the person saw violence at home as the only way to deal with anger. Explain how they might be linked to past circumstances. Use the following list to help you. Start from the present symptom (i.e., behavior on the leaf) and work backward to the root issue. On a sheet of green paper, write what's been done to us (or select from previously prepared sheets), and lay it on floor at feet of tree. Some typical grass-level roots are:

Abandonment, Neglect, Abuse, Anger, Humiliation, Ridicule, What parents did, What parents didn't do, Rejection

TESTIMONY:

Give a brief testimony about how sinful patterns in your life were linked to your personal history.

Testimony Example: My father was very strict and very angry. As a child I never realized that his punishment for me had crossed the line between discipline and physical abuse. I figured that I just was getting what I deserved. Now receiving a spanking isn't wrong in and of itself, but when the paddle is a half-inch thick piece of plywood that I had to make myself and with nails protruding to hurt more but not quite break the skin, then a line has been crossed. Only as an adult did I recognize the trauma that my father inflicted on me. And then I realized that what happened to me helped create unhealthy patterns in my adult life. For example, my father was very emotional and most of that emotion was anger. From that I learned it was wrong to have emotions, so I did my best to shut down all feeling. I also learned that touch is bad because it always involved physical pain. And I see the results now in my marriage where I draw back from physical touch and remain aloof and unconnected emotionally.

 POINT: We cannot stop the symptoms ourselves.

Can we just stop doing the behaviors on our leaves? How many of you have said, "I'll never do that again"—yet end up doing it again? Paul even said it: *"When I want to do good, evil is right there with me"* (Romans 7:21). We all do. It's like trying to get rid of a dandelion. If we just cut off the top but leave the root, it'll just grow back. Same with our lives—if we don't deal with the roots, we'll end up just trying to continually lop off the leaves and watch them grow back over and over again.

POINT: We often feel shame wrongly for what's been done to us.

We're not just ashamed of the leaves on this tree. We're also ashamed of the things that have happened. Satan has us coming and going. Children usually believe that what happens to them is THEIR FAULT. Or perhaps an abuser has told you that. Or you just had to make sense of your environment so you believed that it's your fault. But either way, you're probably ashamed of what happened to you—or what didn't happen that should have.

> **POINT: Underlying our symptoms and what's been done to us are deep, legitimate needs.**

Is that all there is? Or are there reasons for our sins that go deeper than just the grass level? Of course, the answer is yes. Such deep and invisible roots are the needs we're born with. We too easily believe that these roots are what cause our pain, and so we get ashamed of these, too. But these deep roots are legitimate needs that God created in us.

He made us with needs, and he's not ashamed of them.

What is a baby born needing?

Desired Response: Food, shelter, nurture, care, love, stability, mom and dad, protection, God.

BOTTOM LINE: We need to know that when we get up in the morning, the floor will be there, we'll be able to eat and drink and be clothed, and Mom, Dad, and friends will care for us—not beat us up.

Stage: Write these down on brown paper and put the paper on the floor under green papers. Start them as "I need." Typical roots are:

I need love	*I need mom/dad*	*I need food*
I need care	*I need God*	*I need stability*
I need protection/safety	*I need security*	*I need community*
I need to know I'm OK	*I need freedom*	

God created us with these basic needs. It was part of his good plan for us to depend on other people and on himself for these needs. If we had no needs, we wouldn't need anyone—or God. So God knows better...and created us with needs.

If these deep needs aren't met, we'll spend our lives trying to get them taken care of. These needs are like holes in our hearts. Until they are filled up, we just feel empty inside. Sometimes we're inclined to feel that the need itself is bad. "If I hadn't needed so-and-so, then I wouldn't have been abused or neglected or yelled at or made to feel idiotic by him." If we could just get rid of the needs, we think, we'd be in better shape. But God isn't ashamed of our needs. He wants those filled.

TESTIMONY

Arrange for someone to give a brief testimony about how deep needs covered by sinful patterns can be filled once the symptoms are removed.

> *Testimony Example: I thought that my main problem was overeating. Then I understood that I've used food to comfort myself, to cope with pain and loneliness. My whole family did this. And when my mom died, I was overwhelmed with sadness and fear and loneliness. So I turned to food. This is where God is meeting me. As I grieve the loss of my mom, I am learning to not turn to food and to allow God to meet my deep needs for assurance, comfort, and love.*

We're often ashamed of our needs, hurts, and sins.

POINT: We respond with hatred or self-hatred.

And our hearts hurt even more. We're left with one or two possible responses in our hearts—self-hatred or hatred of others. These trap our hearts inside.

> *Stage: Put yellow "self-hatred" or "hatred of others" signs over heart.*

POINT: Healing must start with uncovering shame and turning away from self-hatred.

Shame and self-hatred will keep us from dealing with our problems, behaviors, and issues. They are the first things we have to deal with. (In fact, they are sins and bad habits that we need to get rid of!)

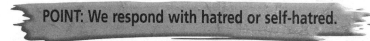 **POINT: Jesus is not ashamed of our needs—nor of us—and wants to help us.**

The situation isn't hopeless. We really need someone to help us. And of course that someone is Jesus. Jesus really wants to help us. He wants to care for us. [To tree volunteer] But when you're covered with all of this, how do we feel? Like being near Jesus? We are ashamed and dirty, weighed down, and far away.

> *Stage: Stand next to the tree and ask this question.*

What are we afraid Jesus will do?
> *Desired Response: cut off limbs, curse the tree, rip off leaves, tell tree it's ugly or bad.*

We might think Jesus wants us to clean up our act so we can come to him. We may fear he'll reject us, punish us, make fun of us, not be there, or not meet the needs. But we forget that Jesus has the soap to clean us up.

If we're afraid of what Jesus will do... then what do we do?
> *Desired Response: Run away, hide, distance ourselves from God and our loved ones, don't look at the issues, deny there's a problem.*

But what does Jesus actually do? Jesus runs to us and hugs us, surrounds us, loves our heart, and heals it. He asks permission, and helps us face our leaves, enables us to drop the bad leaves, and touches roots and heals those. He sees past the leaves and covered heart to who we really are. He washes the shame away.

> *Stage: Jesus approaches gently with permission and takes "shame" off and puts it on the cross. He takes cover off heart and puts it on the cross and removes hatred and gives us a new whole heart instead of a broken one. He hugs and loves the tree. When Jesus comes, he leaves some leaves alone saying, "This can wait a bit." Teaching continues while Jesus cleans all the leaves off the tree.*

Jesus heals our hearts as we open up to him and allow him to meet us and touch us. That's why it's so important to deal with shame. If we stay covered up, we'll never let Jesus meet us. And with self-hatred, if we feel we are unworthy, we'll never expect that Jesus would want to clean us up.

Therefore, there is now no condemnation for those who are in Christ Jesus.—Romans 8:1

WRAP-UP:

We all screw up and hurt others and ourselves. Often this is linked to what's been done to us in the past. And under that are deep needs we all have. When we know that we've screwed up, we get ashamed. Shame covers our symptoms, but also we get ashamed of what's been done to us and of the basic neediness of our own lives.

 POINT: We deal with the different layers in the tree in different ways.

What do we do with the stuff we've done?
  Desired Response: Confess it and get forgiveness.

What about the stuff done to us?
  Desired Response: We forgive what's been done to us.

What about the deep needs?
  Desired Response: We allow Jesus to touch, heal, and meet our deepest needs.

Sounds like the basic Christian life: Confession, forgiveness, forgiving others, looking to God to meet our needs. And it's exactly the basic Christian life that we're talking about.

TREE DIAGRAM

THE POINT: Make personal connections between symptoms, past history, and unmet deep needs.

SUMMARY: Following the pattern laid out in the previous "Tree/Roots" activity, students fill in personal hurts, needs, and sins on individual diagrams.

TIME NEEDED: 5-7 minutes

MATERIALS: Copies of tree diagram (page 28)
Markers or pens

PREPARATION: Have markers and handouts ready.

INTRODUCTION:

What are your needs? What's been done to you? What have you done? What does your tree look like? We all have leaves—sin and unhealthy behavior. We all have hurts—things that have been done to us and things that we wish were done. And we all have really deep needs that we were born with.

Example of a completed "Tree" diagram:

Stage: Pass out tree diagrams.

We're going to spend a few minutes and fill in the tree on your sheet. Name the leaves, the roots, and the unmet needs in your life. Notice where shame and self-hatred have had a significant role. But first let's pray, because we want to focus only on what Jesus wants to deal with right now. He wants to free us and enable some of those leaves or roots to be taken care of. He's not dealing with every one of the 5,694 things that you know are there. He knows about them, but he's not worried about all of those. Right now he's interested in just a few key things—and he'll bring those to mind. After we pray, take this sheet and a write these things down in this picture. (This is just between you and God. You may share these things if you want—and often it's good to have people to share with. But you don't have to.)

POSSIBLE SMALL GROUP QUESTIONS

SMALL GROUP GOALS:

➤ Identify individual needs, sins, and areas of shame.

1. Did you relate to the tree? Were you able to identify any leaves in your life? If you are comfortable, share them.

2. How does it feel to talk about this stuff? How do you feel about the leaves?

3. In what ways do your "leaves" and struggles reveal needs in your heart?

4. Do you know some of the roots connected to those leaves? (surface/grass level)... or deeper ones (the brown "below the surface" ones)...

5. What's been done to you (or what hasn't happened that should have) that caused you pain?

6. How have you covered up or coped with that pain? Does your brokenness make you ashamed?

7. How does it feel to admit needs—the really deep ones?

8. Do the people in your life value appearance and behavior over being real and authentic?

9. In places of neediness, are you aware of how Jesus is FOR you? Do you sometimes feel he's against you? How is admitting your needs to Jesus different and safer than admitting your needs to others?

10. What needs that you've identified would you like us to pray for?

INDIVIDUAL CHALLENGE:

➤ I will allow God to help me look at the real issues and needs in my life.
➤ I will allow God into the real issues and real needs in my life.

RESOURCES AND REFERENCES

RELATED SCRIPTURES:

Matthew 12:33	Romans 7:21-23
Romans 8:1	1 John 1:7-9

OUTSIDE REFERENCE MATERIALS:

Jane Middleton-Moz , *Shame and Guilt: Masters of Disguise* (Health Communications, 1990). Describes how debilitating shame and guilt are created and fostered in childhood and how they manifest themselves in adulthood and intimate relationships.

Gershen Kaufman, Shame: *The Power of Caring* (Schenkman Books, 1992). Written in an informal style that permits the reader to join directly in the exploration, it's a careful examination of how shame so disturbs the functioning of the self that eventually distinct syndromes of shame can develop. These syndromes, rooted in significant interpersonal failure and governed by internalized scenes of shame, cripple self-identity with insecurity, inadequacy, mistrust, and inferiority.

Lewis Smedes, *Shame and Grace: Healing the Shame We Don't Deserve* (HarperCollins, 1994).

Sandra Wilson, *Released from Shame: Recovery for Adult Children of Dysfunctional Families* (People Helper Books) (InterVarsity Press, 1991). Explains the patterns of thinking and feeling common—children of dysfunctional families and helps readers start on their own journey toward freedom and wholeness.

THE REAL PARENT TRAP

GOD IS THE PERFECT PARENT — NOT MOM OR DAD

MAIN POINTS:

1. Our parents shape much of our perception about God.

   ➤ We believe what our parents do more than what they say.

   ➤ How our parents treat us often determines how we view God.

2. When we don't receive what we need from our parents, our world is distorted.

IN THIS LESSON...

Students will understand how

their relationship with their parents

affects how they view God.

FATHER IMAGE

THE POINT: Our understanding of God is often based on our experiences with our parents, but especially fathers or other significant male authority figures. Because they are fallen, human, and sinful, our view of God gets distorted.

SUMMARY: Participants watch and discuss a variety of video clips portraying different types of parents.

TIME NEEDED: 30 minutes

MATERIALS: Video montage of family scenes from movies

PREPARATION: Choose from among the video clips
Cue up video
Copies of worksheet (page 39)

(page 39)

LEADER'S NOTES:

Don't let this lesson degenerate into parent-bashing, which can easily happen if there are kids with very dysfunctional family situations. Be sure to emphasize that this isn't about blaming the parents but about identifying distortions in our perceptions of God. This topic may be difficult for some kids who can't see problems in their families and aren't ready yet to recognize the reality that their parents also are sinful people who mess up and need a savior. Younger teens often want their parents still to be heroes without any faults. Be sensitive to your students as you conduct this session.

INTRODUCTION:

We're going to talk about God's love and care for us—because God is the source of our hope and the power for our healing. All the resources we need spring from him, and the power to change comes only from God. And merely understanding the problem is not enough. It's crucial. But it's only the first step. After understanding that we need God, he can bring change and healing to the pain of our lives.

The real truth, the one that Alcoholics Anonymous tapped into, is that we are indeed helpless and powerless in the face of our brokenness, and only God has the remedy. If we start down any other path we'll end up either relying on our own strength to "just stop" or failing to deal with the real issues and just living with our brokenness.

We are going to be talking about our images of God. Which, believe it or not, start with our parents. So let me ask you this: What's the first thing that you learned from your parents?
Desired Response: To smile, to laugh, to play, to get fed.

Though you don't remember it, from whom did you learn to talk?
Desired Response: Parents. (But be prepared for other answers—grandparent, babysitter, etc.)

How did you learn what was okay to do and what wasn't?
Desired Response: Parents. Although this question is even more likely than the previous one to have alternative answers.

Psychological studies show that our core personality is formed by the time we're 2 years old.

1. **MOVIE:** *Reality Bites*
    SCENE: Dysfunctional Family
    HOW LONG: 2:12
    START: 00:05:03 (dinner scene)
    STOP: 00:07:15 (awkward moment, "Get a Ford.")

2. **MOVIE:** *Father of the Bride*
    SCENE: Father and daughter
    HOW LONG: 2:53
    START: 00:04:14 (monologue in chair)
    STOP: 00:05:27 ("That's when you lose her.")
    START: 00:14:51 (talking with dad, basketball)
    STOP: 00:16:31 (end of song "My Girl")

3. **MOVIE:** *Mr. Holland's Opus*
    SCENE: Father and son
    HOW LONG: 3:53
    START: 00:45:33 (birth of baby)
    STOP: 00:46:26 (kisses wife and smiles at baby)
    START: 01:51:26 (dad coming home)
    STOP: 00:46:26 (sign language of swearing)

4. **MOVIE:** *Hook*
    SCENE: Disappointing dad
    HOW LONG: 2:02
    START: 00:08:26 (Dad with son on plane)
    STOP: 00:08:56 ("But I am a child")
    START: 01:25:20 (smashing clocks with Hook)
    STOP: 01:26:52 ("the place of broken promises")

5. **MOVIE:** *Mr. Mom*
    SCENE: Father and child
    HOW LONG: 2:05
    START: 00:59:22 (talking with son about blanket)
    STOP: 01:01:27 ("May I have a moment to myself?")

6. **MOVIE:** *Strictly Ballroom*
    SCENE: Angry mom, passive dad
    HOW LONG: 2:05
    START: 00:25:30 (mom and dad with Scott)
    STOP: 00:26:25 ("It will be okay Mommy.")
    START: 00:55:30 (talk with mom at 2 a.m.)
    STOP: 00:56:40 (mom slaps son, sister sees)

7. **MOVIE:** *Shine*
    SCENE: Abusive Father
    HOW LONG: 3:15
    START: 00:45:03 (dad confronts and hits son)
    STOP: 00:48:18 ("Don't make me do it.")

POINT: What we learned early in life (about ourselves, our fathers, our mothers, and the world) we generalize and see God through those lenses.

This is much more the case in our emotional selves than in our rational selves. For example, you may know in your mind that God will never leave you or forsake you. But if a parent abandoned you, despite what you know about God's faithfulness, you may have a very hard time actually feeling that God will never leave you and will always be there for you. Your mind understands it, but your heart doesn't believe it.

Let's watch some movie clips that explore relationships between parents and their kids. Some are funny, others are on the intense side.

One big thing to remember before we go any further into this subject: Both parents and children are sinners. Which means you and your parents have failed in one way or another—and will continue to do so. We're not bashing Mom or Dad tonight, but looking honestly at how our parents unconsciously give us our picture of God.

CONTENT:

Stage: Play videos.

Let's summarize the way parents were portrayed in those clips. What were these parents like?

Some desired responses for each clip:

REALITY BITES -	angry, out of touch, meaningless or inappropriate gifts
FATHER OF THE BRIDE -	security in love, lots of communication, enjoy each other, history of fun together
MR. HOLLAND'S OPUS -	tenderness (in baby scene), no attention, no understanding, unimportant, can't relate to child
HOOK -	God's not there, broken promises, no protection
MR. MOM -	lots of respect, communication, wisdom, doesn't talk down, gentle, affirming
STRICTLY BALLROOM -	angry, demanding, manipulative, getting used, not valued, child's feelings ignored, violent
SHINE -	punitive, mixed messages, inconsistent, abusive, violent, guilt trips

POINT: We believe what our parents do more than what they say.

In most of the clips we just saw, what the parent said doesn't match what the parent did. What did the child believe—what the parent said or what the parent did? Now think about the example and actions of your own parents. ✓ What's more credible to you: What they say or what they do?

POINT: The way our parents treat us often influences what we believe about God.

Here's a list of how parents commonly relate to children. Yes, most of them are not pretty. But that's because parents are sinful and kids are sinful and everyone has problems in relationships. My question for you: *How do you think each of these parental behaviors affects our view of God?*

YOUR PROMPT	DESIRED RESPONSE FROM STUDENTS
Dad's busy or not there	God isn't there or doesn't care
Dad is angry or abusive	God is punitive and angry with me
Dad is critical	God is impossible to please
Dad is demanding and a perfectionist	I have to perform to be accepted
Dad doesn't understand feelings	God is distant and unsympathetic
Mom is critical	Love is conditional
Mom wasn't there or bonding was interrupted when you were little	I don't know I'm okay
Mom is demanding	I have to perform to be good
Mom is overprotective or really dominating	I can't make good choices
Mom or Dad affirms performance instead of loving YOU	I work at pleasing
Mom or Dad is moody, depressed (unavailable)	I have to do it all by myself
Mom or Dad is alcoholic or unstable or very unpredictable	I'm not safe, I can't rely on God
Mom or Dad are nurturing	I know I'm taken care of
Mom or Dad love me for who I am, not what I do	I am loved unconditionally
Mom and Dad are very stable and consistent	God is faithful
Mom and Dad discipline carefully	I am thankful for God's discipline
Mom and Dad are there when I need them	I'm sure of God's constant love

Stage: For the following, prompt for as much interaction and response from the group as you can. Keep this moving quickly.

WRAP-UP:

> **POINT: Our views about God are often damaged or limited because of our experience with our fathers and mothers. On some level we believe that God is like our parents.**

TESTIMONY:

Arrange for someone to offer a brief testimony about their parent's impact on them as he or she grew up.

Testimony Example: My father was angry and abusive and constantly belittling. And I was not physically very coordinated. One day, I went into the refrigerator to get some milk and dropped the milk container on floor. It broke open and made a mess. He yelled at me and called me a klutz. That word went all the way into my heart, and I believed that he must have been right about me. As a result I avoided physical challenges especially things requiring good hand-eye coordination or balance. I never went to a dance at school because I knew that I'd be awful at dancing. Only years later, after I forgave my father for the hurtful things he said to me, have I felt I could actually try dancing—and I found I'm actually pretty good at it! It may sound trivial, but it's been a huge thing for me.

Here is the dilemma: God has all the resources we need for our healing and wholeness. But we don't trust God because we don't believe that he's really good, really on our side, really generous, really communicates with us—all because our image of God is warped. So we're cut off from the means to healing.

But here's how we can deal with it: by disconnecting our images of God from what we've heard in our hearts about what God must be like. And we perform this disconnect by hearing from God for ourselves about what he's saying to us. And by letting others help us hear God when we can't hear him on our own.

Some of you may be feeling really angry now—angry about what your parents did or didn't do that hurt you. Maybe you feel depressed or sorry for yourself... maybe you just hurt without any clear reason. I want to pray for you—but after we reflect about our own images of God.

Stage: Distribute repro page (page 39) and give the students a few minutes to fill it out before praying. Then have them form themselves in small groups.

WHAT IS GOD LIKE?

THE POINT: God is a perfect parent to us in every way.

SUMMARY: Participants look at Scriptures to define the type of parent God is.

TIME NEEDED: 10 minutes

MATERIALS: Whiteboard

INTRODUCTION:

There are many ways our thinking about God gets distorted. What's the truth about God? Let's think about what God is like. What are some of the attributes of God that come to mind?

Desired Responses: Loving, all-knowing, powerful, sovereign, holy, just, good, all present, eternal, etc.

Stage: Write them down on whiteboard as people call them out.

Jesus called God his "Father"—and so can we! A father is the human relationship that comes closest to describing our relationship with God. He is our Heavenly Father—not like our earthly ones, but a perfect father.

We can also see snapshots of what God is like by looking at Jesus, who himself said, "He who has seen me has seen the Father."

CONTENT:

This may be hard for you if every image of "Father" is colored by your own experience with your earthly father. But hang in there. If some of what we say produces confusion, anger, or whatever, just note that. It's likely an area that's been hard for you to hear or been an area of pain in your relationship with your own parents.

Also, pay special attention to points that seem too good to be true—they may represent areas in which you need healing.

Stage: In this section, make the point and move along to the next one. Try not to get bogged down, or this can eat a lot of time. Move the following along very quickly.

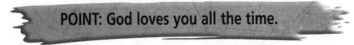

POINT: God loves you all the time.

He is absolutely loving, always, all the time. God is thinking an unending stream of good thoughts toward you all the time. God's love is not punitive or vindictive; he's not trying to get even with us for our sin. He's always patient and kind. Consider how Jesus dealt with the woman caught in adultery, the tax collector, the unbelief and denial of Peter.

"I have loved you with an everlasting love; I have drawn you with loving kindness."
—Jeremiah 31:3

POINT: God is faithful.

He is consistently loving—he never changes in his desire for us. He knew us before we were born and has watched over us every second of our lives. Even in your painful and tragic times, he's been present. You grow up from your parents and eventually leave and become adults. Even when you've "graduated" from your household, you never "graduate" from God. God is always there, he will never leave us, he is our perfect parent forever.

"I will never desert you, nor will I ever forsake you." —Hebrews 13:5
"I am with you always even to the end of the age." —Matthew 28.20
"If we are faithless, he will remain faithful. For he can not disown himself."
—2 Timothy 2:13

POINT: God is generous.

God is not a stingy God withholding blessing from his children. See how extravagant he is in creation—the beauty of crystals, flowers, and gems. His desire is big—for all creation, for every person, for the whole world. He gives blessing in abundance and never is unwilling to give to us—even when he knows we'll mess up with it.

"God is able to make all grace abound to you so that in all things at all times, having all that you need, you will abound in every good work. Now he who supplies seed to the sower and bread for food will also supply and increase your store of seed and will enlarge the harvest of your righteousness. You will be made rich in every way so that you can be generous on every occasion."
—2 Corinthians 9:8

POINT: God is pleased with us.

He's proud of us. Have you ever seen a father boasting about his son? How about God—with Jesus at his baptism...with Job in heaven. We are sons and daughters of God, and he's pleased with us. He knows us and knows what we can and can't do—he will not push us beyond our limit. (Matthew 3:16-17, Job 42:7-17)

POINT: God has a plan for us.

He has plans for us that he wants us to walk in.
"For I know the plans I have for you, declares the Lord, plans to prosper you and not to harm you. Plans to give you a hope and a future." —Jeremiah 29:11

He will never give up on these plans. He intends freedom for us.

"The Lord sets prisoners free, the Lord gives sight to the blind, the Lord lifts up those who are bowed down." —Psalm 146:7-8

POINT: God is able.

"It's not like God is willing but unable! We don't have a weak God. Our God is patient and forbearing. Among all the miracles he did, He raised Jesus (and others) from the dead." —Ephesians 1:18-20

POINT: God disciplines out of love.

God isn't at all like the permissive parent who doesn't know what to do with his kids or is too afraid of their reactions to set limits. God isn't at all like the abusive parent who hurts his children whenever he feels like it. No, God disciplines the ones he loves—and he disciplines us lovingly, not angrily. Though his discipline may hurt at times, it's for our good.

"Our fathers disciplined us for a little while as they thought best; but God disciplines for our good, that we may share in his holiness. No discipline seems pleasant at the time, but painful. Later on, however, it produces a harvest of righteousness and peace for those who have been trained by it." —Hebrews 12:10-11

WRAP-UP:

God has all the resources we need for our healing and wholeness. He knows who we really are and loves us absolutely. He wants to pour out blessings on us, his children, and set us free from our sin. We need to trust God for our healing and ask him for his strength, power, and love.

LEADER'S NOTES:

As a follow up to this session, you might want encourage kids for their personal devotional times to do a further study on what Scripture says about God's character.

POSSIBLE SMALL GROUP QUESTIONS

SMALL GROUP GOALS:

Discuss how our images of our parents affects our image of God

1. How does your relationship with your parents affect your relationship with God?

2. How does your mom or dad model what God is like?

3. What's the biggest way they're different from God?

4. When you think about the different aspects of God's character we discussed, what seems too good to be true or hard to believe? Why?

5. In what ways do you need to see God in a new light?

6. How can we pray?

INDIVIDUAL CHALLENGE:

I will disconnect my feelings about God from my feelings about my parents.

I will allow God to meet my need for a Father.

RESOURCES AND REFERENCES

RELATED SCRIPTURES:

2 Corinthians 9:8
Hebrews 12:10-11
Hebrews 13:15
Jeremiah 29:11
Jeremiah 31:3
Matthew 7:11
Matthew 28:20
Psalm 146:7-8
Romans 8:15-17
Matthew 3:16-17
Job 42:7-17
2 Timothy 2:13

OUTSIDE REFERENCE MATERIALS:

John Dawson, *The Father Heart of God* (American Tract Society, 2000).
Excellent and brief consideration of God's heart toward us. Terrific for follow-up devotional study.

IT'S EASY FOR ME TO SEE GOD LIKE THIS:

BECAUSE MY PARENTS ARE LIKE THIS:

IT'S HARD FOR ME TO SEE GOD LIKE THIS:

BECAUSE, IN MY FAMILY, I LEARNED:

HE LOVES ME, HE LOVES ME NOT

LEARNING HOW TO RECEIVE (AND KEEP) GOD'S AMAZING LOVE

MAIN POINTS:

1. We all have a foundational need to know we are loved.

2. There are blocks to our ability to receive love from God.

3. We need the chance to simply BE with God.

4. Lack of early bonding often creates a void.

  - That void can make it hard to accept love.

  - We may have trouble just being with God.

5. God wants to fill that void with the ability to receive his love, a sense of peace, and a sense that "it's okay to be me."

LESSON SEGMENTS:

Cups
Making Our Own Cups

IN THIS LESSON...

Receiving God's love...

Getting still to simply BE with God...

Inviting Jesus to meet our needs...

CUPS

THE POINT: Our hearts cry out for unconditional acceptance.

SUMMARY: A series of cups with varying numbers of holes is used to describe the way past hurts keep us from "holding" the love that God and others pour into us.

TIME NEEDED: 35 minutes

MATERIALS:
2 cardboard cartons full of liquid
Large bowl or tray for pouring liquid
3 paper cups or containers:
(1 cup, top covered with plastic wrap)
(1 cup, no holes)
(1 cup, some holes)
Strainer

PREPARATION: Prepare cartons
Prepare cups

INTRODUCTION:

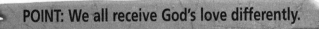

POINT: We all receive God's love differently.

Stage: Invite a student volunteer to join you at the front of the room. Over a bowl, the student will pour lemonade, water, or colored water into each container as you describe each situation.

Sometimes we're full of God's love.

Stage: Pour into cup with no holes.

Other times we leak.

Stage: Pour into cup with a few holes.

Other times we have things in the way and can't receive love.

Stage: Pour onto cup covered with plastic wrap.

And sometimes we feel like we have no capacity to hold love at all.

Stage: Pour into a strainer.

POINT: We can't always receive God's love.

Our souls are like these containers—and usually one of the damaged ones. God pours in love, but we can't always receive it. Or, if we can receive it, we can't accept it for long.

What kinds of things make holes in our hearts so we can't accept God's love for us?
Desired Response: Allow for discussion about how past hurts and getting burned in relationships with others make it hard to trust anyone, etc.

These things all play a part. It goes deeper, though. Research tells us that most of our ability to just be and receive love is formed by the time we're just 1 or 2 years old! And a lot of it comes from our first and primary relationship—Mom. It's part of the love she gives. From our mothers, we receive a sense of security, a sense that we're okay. This sets us up for the rest of our lives to be okay in the world.

What kinds of things can a baby learn from its relationship with Mom? What does a baby learn when the mother holds, kisses, feeds, and cares for the baby?
Desired Response: I am loved, I am important, I am cared for, I am safe, someone is there for me.

All these things develop our sense of being—our sense of well-being and security that helps us receive and accept love.

What effect would it have on the baby (and the baby's ability to accept love) if the mom relationship was somehow interrupted? For example, if the newborn must spend lots of time in the hospital…if the mom is physically or emotionally sick…if the baby is juggled between foster families…etc.

Desired Response: The baby wouldn't learn that it's secure and safe, and it wouldn't develop a good sense of being.

What is the opposite of being? Yes, doing! Many people who don't have a strong sense of being live life trying to do things to earn people's love, rather that being able to simply receive love. Remember the story of Jesus visiting Mary and Martha for dinner?

LEADER'S NOTES:

If students aren't familiar with it, read this story in Luke 10:38-41 or summarize it.

Martha ran around trying to do things to earn Jesus' approval and love, while Mary was able to just sit and be with Jesus. Martha's cup probably had a lot more holes in it than Mary's did.

At the end of the story, Jesus tells the sisters that Mary had chosen the better way—that is, sitting with him, conversing with him…not running around in the kitchen. Jesus tells us the same thing, too. It's better for us to learn to sit and BE with Jesus rather than trying to earn his love.

POINT: We need to simply BE with God.

"Be still and know that I am God."—Psalm 46:10

We must be still and…BE. But our culture and backgrounds thwart that. Culture says it isn't cool to just be…we have to DO all the time. Heaven forbid we should go anywhere without staying in cell-phone and pager range! We're often too busy to have relationships. We're all harried and often take little time to be still with God. He has lots to say to us, but we often just can't sit still and listen.

WRAP-UP:

How does this relate to us?

What kind of doing do we tend to value as a culture?

> *Desired Response: Noise, productivity, getting stuff done, working long hours.*

How do you feel when you don't have access to your e-mail or cell phone?

> *Desired Response: Out of touch.*

Other cultures view time in very different ways. Here in the U.S., time is always critical; but in Latin American cultures, for example, they tend to value relationships more than time or efficiency. In Mexico, when you come to a meeting, you may spend a great deal of time simply greeting each other—then, after relationships are established or renewed, business can take place.

 POINT: Our ability to receive God's love is often blocked.

Jesus wants to give us relationship and permission to simply BE.

4 things can affect BEING with Jesus…

1. *It's culturally uncool.* We have to have the cell phone, e-mail, and pager available all the time, to fill every quiet moment with noise.

2. *Our relationships with our parents, especially Mom.* Fathers tend to give us a sense of protection, strength, and affirmation, but our mothers often give us nurture, stability, and unconditional love—in short, a sense of BEING. And if it doesn't happen early in life, it may not happen at all. The importance of this mother-child bonding cannot be overestimated. Generally it's your mother who lets you know that it's okay to be yourself, it's okay that you exist, that you have a voice, that you are you.

3. *Trauma or interruptions during the process of early development* (e.g., violence, abuse, addiction, repeated chaos, neglect, or instability).

4. *We think we don't deserve God's love.* Just like the Prodigal Son in Jesus' parable, we believe that after what we've done, there's no way that God would love us.

TESTIMONY:

Arrange for someone to offer a brief testimony about lack of early bonding and the impact it has in later life.

Testimony Example: My mom wasn't an easy person to live with...at least not for a sensitive and perfectionist child like me. There was only one right way to do things—hers. And there was always something wrong with how I acted or did things. Consequently, I grew up without a real closeness to her. As I reached adulthood, I learned that I didn't want to be anything like her. But this left me without the very good things she did—and with a major hole in my life. Unable to rest, I had to strive for perfection and had few close friends to reflect God's encouragement. I was left lonely, unable to receive love (especially from women, who, of course, seemed more critical than men). Strong women seemed to run over me like steamrollers. I wanted their affection and approval, but they annihilated who I was. It wasn't until later that I forgave my mom and began to accept the things about me that were like her. It allowed me to receive more of God's love, and properly receive his love offered through women around me.

Again, this isn't about bashing our parents. No parent is perfect, no parent gives a child everything that child needs. What this lesson is about is the importance of knowing what we received and didn't receive from our parents. And Jesus can heal us even if we received the wrong stuff, or if we got too little of the good stuff.

Even the best parents can't be perfect—we're all sinful. When we become parents, we won't be perfect, either. And even if parents were perfect and poured perfect love and affection into their kids, kids often ignore love, or they'll receive it inappropriately, because they're imperfect, too.

POINT: We bear the results of our lack of early bonding with our parents.

What happens when Mom and Dad can't or don't provide this love? There are often consequences–

- We may be hyperactive or constantly fidgeting, unable to be still or quiet.

- Reacting against Mom, we may be unable to receive love from her.

- This may result in unhealthy sexual behavior.

- Deprived of parental love, a person may develop a need for "mother love"—which can manifest itself through cross-dressing, a fascination with and sexualized need for women, homosexuality, breast fetishes, etc.

- This can lead to a demand for touch—which, though very human and necessary and legitimate in and of itself—can, in the extreme, lead to promiscuity springing from that basic touch deprivation.

- We may not be able to be still and receive God's love.

- We may struggle with self-hatred.

- We may feel an emptiness inside us that never gets filled.

- We may feel deep needs for others' approval so we can "feel okay" or so they can tell us who we "are."

- We may become emotionally dependent—looking to other people to fill our empty places, only to find they can't be filled at all…and, sometimes, that even God can't fill the hole.

WRAP-UP:

POINT: Jesus can heal our deep, unmet needs.

Jesus can heal this stuff. He wants to bring hope. If this is pain that goes back to deprivations during your infancy, then it's really deep—but it's much easier for Jesus to heal that pain if we first acknowledge that it's there. And when we do acknowledge that pain, it can feel like an unfillable hole. The pain must come up and out so Jesus can fill and heal it.

Romans 8:38-39 reminds us that *"neither death nor life, neither angels nor demons, nor any powers, neither height nor depth, nor anything else in all creation will be able to separate us from the love of God that is in Christ Jesus our Lord."* Take comfort in that promise!

MAKING OUR OWN CUPS

THE POINT: To respond by making our own cups to represent our personal ability to receive love.

TIME NEEDED: 10 minutes

MATERIALS:
Cups
Scissors
Tape
Markers
Construction paper
Plastic wrap

INTRODUCTION:

Let's take some time to think about the state of our own lives and how able we are to receive God's love. We'll each decorate our own cups to show at what level we feel we're able to receive love—and maybe symbolize some of the barriers in the way of our receiving God's love.

CONTENT:

Stage: Have group make their own cups and share in small groups. Then students can pray for one another to be able to receive God's healing in their lives and receive more of his love for them.

POSSIBLE SMALL GROUP QUESTIONS

SMALL GROUP GOALS:

- Share about being vs. doing.
- Pray that God will fill the initial sense of being.

1. What does your cup look like?
2. Are you more oriented to "being" or "doing"?
3. Is it harder for you to do something *for* God or to simply *be* with him?
4. Which container or cup do you identify with the most? Why?
5. What things do you feel you received sufficiently when you were very young—e.g., nurture, stability, unconditional love, etc.?
6. What things do you think were missing?
7. Was your early relationship with your parents—that is, your bonding with your parents—ever interrupted?
8. How is your "sense of being"?
9. How can we pray for you?

INDIVIDUAL CHALLENGE:

- I will spend time just "being" with God and worshiping him.

RESOURCES AND REFERENCES

RELATED SCRIPTURES:

Psalm 46:10
Zephaniah 3:17
Luke 10:38-41
Romans 8:38-39

OUTSIDE REFERENCE MATERIALS:

Leanne Payne, *The Healing Presence: Curing the Soul through Union with Christ* (Baker, 1995). Excellent foundational work, but be prepared for some serious thinking.

Leanne Payne, *Restoring the Christian Soul: Overcoming Barriers to Completion in Christ through Healing Prayer* (Baker, 1996). Especially chapter 8, "Prolonged healing of profound pain."

Lori Rentzel, *Emotional Dependency* (InterVarsity Press, 1991). Highly recommended. There's a brief treatment of a very common issue, especially for women.

WHO DO YOU THINK YOU'RE FOOLING?

REMOVING THE FACADES AND LIVING CONFIDENTLY AS THE REAL YOU

MAIN POINTS:

1. Deep insecurities often make us feel we're not okay.

2. We base our self-worth on others' opinions.

3. Therefore, in an attempt to get others to love us, we begin wearing masks.

4. We spend a lot of our energy constructing and buttressing these masks.

5. We believe we must deny our own feelings of inadequacy, otherwise the negative thoughts will weaken us.

6. When we remove our masks, we trust God to show us our true identity.

IN THIS LESSON...

Learning about our masks...

Letting down our masks (and getting real with Jesus)...

Finding Jesus' strength and love
so we can be real with others...

LESSON SEGMENTS:

What Role Am I Playing?
Making Masks

"WHAT ROLE AM I PLAYING?"

THE POINT: There are common roles we all play in relationships.

SUMMARY: Participants perform role-plays that represent different masks people wear.

TIME NEEDED: 40 minutes

MATERIALS: Copies of the **Improvisation Role Plays** (pages 54-55)
Video of *Wizard of Oz*

ROLES NEEDED: Group is made up of improv actors for a series of sketches

PREPARATION: Cue video to where the wizard's purely human identity is revealed by Toto.
Start: 1:27:10 (Dorothy returns to Wizard with broom)
Stop: 1:28:58 (Wizard "… just a bad wizard")
Make enough copies of **Improvisation Role Plays** to hand out.
Write all the roles on whiteboard.

INTRODUCTION:

Stage: Show Wizard of Oz *clip.*

 POINT: We all construct masks for ourselves.

What is it we're trying to hide? Our true selves, usually. We fear that if people know who we really are that we would be rejected or hurt. We say to ourselves, "If this or that person really knew me, she wouldn't like me." So we want to hide behind something to protect ourselves.

What is it we want others to see? Probably something they'll like, or at least respect, so they won't reject us (we think). We spend a lot of time and energy keeping up these images.

We can spend all our time and energy constructing masks. To look right, sound right, walk right, talk right, dress right, hang with the right people, etc. Pretty soon we care more about keeping up the images than about who we really are.

POINT: We believe we can't allow ourselves to think negative thoughts—so we deny our feelings.

This isn't just an outward show—we can't allow even our own thoughts about ourselves get in the way of our image. Sometimes we even force our feelings inside to match the mask. For example, if my image is "super-cool," I won't ever let myself feel negative or vulnerable feelings. After all, if those feelings sneak out, then my image is blown!

We try to push down the "bad" feelings (fear, anger, hurt, doubt, guilt) and only experience "good" feelings, because (we think) it's simply wrong of us to have bad feelings. Haven't we all said, "That's okay" or "I'm fine!" when we were actually dying inside? This is merely denying how we're really feeling.

TESTIMONY:

Arrange for someone to offer a brief testimony about not allowing yourself to feel.

Testimony Example: I always believed that if people really knew me down deep then they wouldn't like me. So I put on this outward show in order to be sure that no one could see the real me and reject me. I decided that for me to get people to like me, I had to be happy all the time and not ask anything of them. Not a good way to live. Freedom for me came when I finally allowed God first to see me as I was (as if he didn't know me all along!) and then had the courage to allow others to see the real me.

POINT: Shame and deep insecurity are at the root of the need to cover up.

What's going on underneath? Why are we so hung up about what others think?
Desired Response: We're insecure; others' opinions are powerful…

If we're insecure about who we are, we'll always look to others to tell us who we are. If our sense of worth is dependent only on what others say or think about us, then we'll show them our masks in order to receive affirmation. Ancient mythology tells the story of Narcissus. Does anyone know who he fell in love with? Himself! Narcissus fell in love with his own image reflected in a pond.

Which is where we get the words *narcissism* and *narcissistic*, words that describe people who are obsessed with themselves, usually because they are so insecure about who they are on the inside. It's all about the image. The narcissists' masks reflect their insecurity. The more exaggerated the mask, the more desperate the insecurity. Narcissism is wearing a mask...all image and no inward solidity.

WRAP-UP:

POINT: Masks are a manipulative attempt to control others' feelings about us.

We make masks—false images of ourselves—to manipulate or control our relationships. These protect our vulnerabilities. Sometimes they're gentle and passive and don't make waves...sometimes they are violent and angry, in order to keep others at a distance through fear.

When we put on the same mask over and over, we set a pattern or habit for how we are relating. This becomes like the role in a play that we continually act out. We're going to play a game to illustrate these very common and recognizable roles.

Stage:

- *Have your group split up into pairs, except for one group of three.*
- *Distribute one role-play suggestion slip to each pair, and give the group of three the "Clown" role-play*
- *Each group has 5 minutes to come up with a 1-minute sketch to illustrate one of the roles we play to protect ourselves or control others.*
- *Write out the 8 roles on the whiteboard (Good Kid, Tough Kid, Angry Kid, Party Kid, Clown, Victim, Fixer, Seducer), though not in performance order. Tell kids to refer to this list to figure out what role a given role-play is illustrating.*
- *At the end of each sketch, have the rest of the group guess each of the roles.*

LEADER'S NOTES:

Improv is a great tool to get kids engaged with a topic. Though not necessarily for shy kids. So be sensitive to the kids in your group. Encourage participation, match shy kids with the extroverts, and start and end each sketch with applause to affirm their mere willingness to get up and try it.

CONTENT:

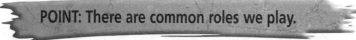

POINT: There are common roles we play.

Stage: After the sketches are performed, discuss the roles in each one. Lead the group into defining each role. They may look something like this:

PARTY KID: "What me worry? Life is a party, just have fun and don't let anything get to you."

GOOD KID: "I follow all the rules, so no one will ever get mad at me."

TOUGH KID: "I'll hurt you before you hurt me."

CLOWN: Cracks jokes, always funny; everyone likes (or laughs at) the Clown.

VICTIM: Someone or something else always causes problem, real or imaged

FIXER: Always focused on others to keep attention away.

ANGRY: Constantly blows up, makes people afraid of getting an angry reaction. Best defense is a good offense.

SEDUCER: Always flirting and interacting sexually. Constantly looking for attention from the opposite sex. Maybe trying to seem more "experienced" than they really are.

Other possible roles include (but aren't limited to)
CHECKED OUT, DEPRESSED, SNOB, QUIET, JOCK, GOTH, PREPPY, DRUGGIE

TESTIMONY:

Arrange for someone to offer a brief testimony about a role they played.

Testimony Example: Sarcasm was the role I played. I became the master of the quick and cutting one-liner. Funny, but always at someone's expense and always putting someone down. And I used that as a defense mechanism to keep others away, and for me to stay in the superior position. It worked to keep others away, but not because they all thought I was so smart—they just didn't want to be around someone so insulting and arrogant. The reality under the covers was that I was deeply hurt and didn't know how to deal with it. By being always sarcastic I could keep other people who wanted to get closer to me away and stay safe. But inside I was desperately lonely and afraid to admit it.

Masks can be quite elaborate—and they can get you into trouble.

Take seductiveness, for example—if you need to find affirmation from others, you may try to appear as sexually tempting as possible in order to get attention. This manipulates others by pushing their sexual buttons.

These are all ways that we cover over our hearts to protect ourselves.

POINT: God sees through masks and asks us to come to him in honesty.

God sees through the masks—but we have a choice. Do you want to spend your time and energy constructing a false image or developing the real you? Being real before God and with each other is the first step. This can be really scary—God calls us to confess our sins to one another (James 5:16). Small groups are a good place to start. God wants to build a community of his people who are willing to share ALL of their lives together.

Some scriptures about masks:

"Put away all deceit, hypocrisy, envy and slander of every kind." —1 Peter 2:1

"We have renounced secret and shameful ways, we do not use deception, nor do we distort the Word of God." —2 Corinthians 4:2

"Now the Lord is the Spirit, and where the Spirit of the Lord is, there is freedom. And we, who with unveiled faces all reflect the Lord's glory, are being transformed into his likeness with ever-increasing glory, which come from the Lord, who is the Spirit." —2 Corinthians 3:17-18

MAKING YOUR MASK

THE POINT: We need to identify the masks we hide behind.

SUMMARY: Participants make their own masks to represent false images they portray.

TIME NEEDED: 15 minutes

MATERIALS: Blank masks for all, copied or printed on construction paper or card stock
Markers
Scissors
Tape
Elastic thread (available at sewing or craft stores)
—about 12 inches per mask
Stapler

PREPARATION: Cut out masks including eyeholes and, using a stapler, attach the elastic thread to hold mask on. (If you want kids to do this as part of the session, then add 5 minutes to your time.)
You should prepare a mask of your own as an example to share with kids when you get to that interaction.

INTRODUCTION:

We're going to make some masks tonight. These are our own stories of what we've put on to try to hide behind.

CONTENT:

Stage: Set out markers and masks. Have students create their own masks.

WRAP-UP:

We don't have to hide behind masks before God or with each other. Let's talk in small groups about the masks we've hidden behind. And then we'll come back as a large group for some final worship—and to take off our masks and put them on the cross. This means we're not going to spend any more time trying to impress others with our false images—that we are committing to be real, honest people with God and with each other.

Finally, it means that we're no longer going to try to protect ourselves, but that we'll lay down our defenses before God and trust him to protect us.

Stage: After small groups are done, pray for the large group that God will become our guard and protector as we lay our masks down before him. (See prayer below for ideas.) In worship, ask each person to remove his/her mask and lay it at the cross or hang it on the cross.

PRAYER BEFORE OR AFTER TAKING OFF MASKS:

Lord, we want to take off our masks before you. We confess that we've used these to hold up false images of who we really are and to manipulate others' opinions of us. We confess that we've used masks as ways to protect our hearts from rejection, and we now trust you to protect our hearts. We renounce the images that may seem more real than who we really are! Give us the courage to walk free from them and to be who we really are before you and others. Help us not to be ashamed to be weak, hurting, or sinful but to recognize your love for us in the middle of our sin. And we choose now to let you be our protector—the One who guards our hearts with your Spirit. In Jesus' name, Amen.

POSSIBLE SMALL GROUP QUESTIONS

SMALL GROUP GOALS:
- Discuss the masks we've made.
- Pray to renounce masks as our identities and allow Jesus to form his identity in us.

1. What mask did you draw? How does it represent you?
2. What do you do to make sure other people like you?
3. Does not liking yourself relate to wearing certain masks? How so?
4. Do you find yourself needing to be something for others that you really aren't?
5. God loves you and wants the very best for you. How is wearing a mask NOT God's best for you? How does it limit you and your relationships?
6. God loves you as a sinner. But do you? Why is it hard to love yourself?

INDIVIDUAL COMMITMENT:
- I will begin to take off my mask and live transparently, trusting God to protect me.

RESOURCES AND REFERENCES

RELATED SCRIPTURE:
2 Corinthians 3:17-18
2 Corinthians 4:2
1 Peter 2:1

OUTSIDE REFERENCE MATERIALS:

Alexander Lowen, *Narcissism: Denial of the True Self* (Touchstone Books, 1997).

Jane Middleton-Moz, *Shame and Guilt: Masters of Disguise* (1990). Describes how debilitating shame and guilt are created and fostered in childhood and how they manifest themselves in adulthood and intimate relationships.

"WHAT ROLE AM I PLAYING?"
IMPROVISATION ROLE PLAYS

GOOD KID

CHARACTERISTICS:

Lives up to all the rules.

Never causes problems.

Obeys parents, teachers and other authority figures.

POSSIBLE SKETCH IDEAS:

"Good Kid" talks with a friend about skipping class.

Friend wants "Good Kid" to go out Saturday and get drunk.

Girlfriend or boyfriend wants to stay out all night when "Good Kid" has a curfew.

TOUGH KID

CHARACTERISTICS:

"I'll hurt you before you hurt me."

Aggressive and angry.

Bossy and always in charge.

POSSIBLE SKETCH IDEAS:

Dad tells "Tough Kid" that his curfew is now 10 p.m. on Friday. "Tough Kid" gets angry and tells off his dad.

"Tough Kid" gets dumped by boyfriend or girlfriend—gets angry and trashes the room and the ex.

"Tough Kid" wants to get his friend to go to a ball game, but the friend wants to go home. "Tough Kid" wants to be the big boss.

PARTY KID

CHARACTERISTICS:

No worries.

Wants to play around all the time.

He's a friend only when things are fun and easy; when times get tough, he's outta there.

POSSIBLE SKETCH IDEAS:

A friend tries to get "Party Kid" to talk about college major and what to do for a job. "Party Kid" doesn't want to think about the future.

ANGRY KID

CHARACTERISTICS:

Constantly blows up.

Makes people afraid of getting an anger reaction.

Believes the best defense is a good offense.

POSSIBLE SKETCH IDEAS:

"Angry Kid" gets caught cheating on a test by the teacher.

"Angry Kid" gets stood up by a date-to-be, who later calls "Angry Kid."

IMPROVISATION ROLE PLAYS

THE CLOWN (3 PEOPLE)

CHARACTERISTICS:

Constantly cracks jokes
Always acting goofy
Everyone likes him or her

POSSIBLE SKETCH IDEAS:

Someone has just heard about a death in the family, and the "Clown" starts telling jokes, hoping to make the person feel better. Of course, the jokes—not to mention the idea of joking at a time like this—are inappropriate.

It's graduation and the "Clown" has to do something at an awards dinner. The "Clown" is talking with friends about plans. It gets bizarre.

Mom and Dad are fighting and the "Clown" tries to get them to stop by cutting jokes.

VICTIM

CHARACTERISTICS:

Assumes blame for problems, even when he or she is not at all to blame
Depressed, lots of self-pity
Self-centered and self-absorbed

POSSIBLE SKETCH IDEAS:

Mom gets home late from work, is stressed out about being late for an evening appointment, date, errand, etc. She blames the "Victim" for her lateness, and the "Victim" meekly accepts the accusation.

In a fight with a girlfriend or boyfriend, the "Victim" is blamed for the other's flirting habit.

FIXER

CHARACTERISTICS:

Always focuses and tries to repair others' problems
Downplays his or her own problems

POSSIBLE SKETCH IDEAS:

A friend calls the "Fixer" about an impending divorce in the friend's family; "Fixer" gives suggestions on how the divorce can be stopped.

After a friend is dumped, the "Fixer" tries to make the friend feel better by downplaying the friend's responsibility in the break-up.

SEDUCER

CHARACTERISTICS:

Looking for attention from the opposite sex
Flirty and suggestive in speech, clothing, manner
Weak personal boundaries—not respecting his or her own body or emotions…
nor those of the desired other

POSSIBLE SKETCH IDEAS:

A friend (the "Seducer" insists it's "just a friend") calls the "Seducer," who wants to get invited out to a picnic for the weekend.

The "Seducer" starts flirting with a member of the opposite sex in the school cafeteria.

I WANT YOU, I NEED YOU

LEARNING HOW TO WORSHIP THE CREATOR INSTEAD OF THE CREATED

5

MAIN POINTS:

1. An idol is something from which we get our identity other than God.

- Emotional dependency is a form of relational idolatry—"I need someone else to be complete."

2. If we let idols rules us, they can destroy us.

- We have idols because we try to fill our needs in the wrong places.

- If we keep following idols, we'll become like them.

- Our goal is to stand straight and get our identity in Jesus.

- Jesus gives us the power to renounce our idols.

LESSON SEGMENTS:

Idols Movie Clips
Love Fool
Making Idols

IN THIS LESSON...

Identifying the "idols" in your life...

Finding out about how relationships can become idols...

Smashing your idols (literally) and
turning to Jesus for identity...

IDOLS MOVIE CLIPS

THE POINT: Idols are things we don't feel we can live without.

SUMMARY: Participants watch and discuss a variety of video clips that illustrate different idols people worship.

TIME NEEDED: Will vary

MATERIALS: Video clips containing images of idols.

> *Indiana Jones and the Temple of Doom*
> *Major League*
> *Varsity Blues*
> *Jerry Maguire*
> *The Nutty Professor*
> *Wayne's World*
> *Almost Famous*
> *Say Anything*

PREPARATION: After previewing these (or similar) clips, decide which ones are appropriate for the lesson and your group—then cue 'em up.

LEADER'S NOTES:

The following array of clips give a good variety of examples of different types of idolatry. However, due to time constraints, money constraints, availability, or concern over content, you may not choose to use all of these clips. In that case, choose the 3 or 4 clips that most accurately reflect the types of idolatry that kids in your group are dealing with.

The clip from *Say Anything* really leads into the topic of emotional dependency —a major issue for many kids, especially girls.

MOVIE: *Indiana Jones and the Temple of Doom*
SCENE: Worshippers of Kali in cave temple with huge skull
HOW LONG: 30 seconds
START TIME: 1:01:00
STOP TIME: 1:31:00 (pan up and freeze on skull idol)

MOVIE: *Major League* (NOTE: profanity is used in this clip.)
SCENE: Baseball player sacrifices to "Jobu" so he can hit curve balls
HOW LONG: 1:05
START TIME: 00:18:59
STOP TIME: 00:20:14 ("Are you trying to say Jesus Christ can't hit a curve ball?")

MOVIE: *Varsity Blues* (NOTE: strong use of profanity; the F word is prominent)
SCENE: Football title is an idol (2 scenes)
HOW LONG: 1:00 and 1:08
FIRST CLIP START TIME: Beginning narration about the town loving football, doing what it takes
1ST CLIP STOP TIME: After the narration that ends, "Win at all costs"
2ND CLIP START TIME: 1:26:28 (team confronts coach about winning at all costs)
2ND CLIP STOP TIME: 1:27:36 ("All you care about is your next district title.")

MOVIE: *Jerry Maguire* (NOTE: profanity is used.)

SCENE: Money/success is an idol

HOW LONG: 1:30

START TIME: 00:27:02 (football player tells Jerry, "Show me the money!")

STOP TIME: 00:28:32 (office staff looks strangely at Jerry after he screams, "Show me the money!")

MOVIE: *The Nutty Professor* (NOTE: offensive language is used.)

SCENE: Body image as idol

HOW LONG: 2:16

START TIME: 00:34:45 (professor drinks potion and becomes thin, obsesses over his weight loss)

STOP TIME: 00:37:01 ("Spandex, all spandex, where's the spandex section?")

MOVIE: *Wayne's World*

SCENE: Idolizing Alice Cooper

HOW LONG: 00:52

START TIME: 1:01:00

STOP TIME: 1:31:00 ("We are scum, we suck.")

MOVIE: *Almost Famous*

SCENE: Music idols--"Robert Plant signed my T-shirt..."

HOW LONG: 00:32

START TIME: 32:40

STOP TIME: 33:12

MOVIE: *Almost Famous*

SCENE: Idolizing fame, self, and partying: "I am a golden god!"

HOW LONG: 1:23

START TIME: 57:17

STOP TIME: 58:40

MOVIE: *Say Anything*

SCENE: Relational idolatry

HOW LONG: 00:38 seconds

START TIME: 00:23:16

STOP TIME: 00:23:54 ("Did Joe come here with Mimi?" girl nods)

INTRODUCTION:

Stage: Read the following.

from Exodus 20: 3-6 (The Ten Commandments)
"You shall have no other gods before me. You shall not make for yourself an idol in the form of anything in heaven above or on the earth beneath or in the waters below. You shall not bow down to them or worship them; for I, the LORD your God, am a jealous God, punishing the children for the sin of the fathers to the

third and fourth generation of those who hate me, but showing love to a thousand generations of those who love me and keep my commandments."

What is an idol?
Desired Response: Have group name biblical idols but move to current examples as well.

There are lots of examples of idols out there. Since movies are all around us, let's look at some images of idols in our culture—from the movies.

CONTENT:

Stage: Play the video clips you decided to use.

Now what kind of idols did you just see in those clips?

Stage: Talk about what you saw, and what or who was idolized in each clip. Keep this brief.

What do you think of this definition? An idol is anything we attach to or that gives us our identity other than God.
An idol is anything about which we say, "I can't live without —" or "I'm nothing without —." Idols are related to identity. They are something we want to be like or copy. Think of an idol as something you can't live without, beyond our basic human needs of basic foods (as opposed to too much food), clothing to cover us and shelter, and love. Even those essential things can become idols if we love them more than is right.

> **POINT: An idol is anything that we look to for our identity.**

What can be idols? What do they look like? What did we see in the movie clips?

Stage: Have the group break up into groups of three and identify the three top things their culture idolizes. Ask each trio to call them out. Or call for students' thoughts in a large group, without breaking it up.

Desired Response: Girlfriends, boyfriends, money, sex, power, popularity, music, fame, etc.

Stage: Write down some of the idols as they are suggested.

What are the consequences of setting up and "following" an idol—that is, letting it rule you?

Stage: Have group suggest simple, typical consequences of following two or three of the idols the group listed. Then select one or two of the idols and lead your group toward exploring deeper consequences. Suggest a typical story line of an idolatrous situation, and ask the group to fill in the plot elements. Suggest twists of plot if you need to urge your group along to understanding that when we serve idols, we're likely to be led away from God.

For example: If a girl idolizes her boyfriend…
- *She might get so obsessed that she ignores her friends (and consequently loses them). What happens when she finally breaks up with her boyfriend? She finds herself friendless and alone.*
- *She might put the boyfriend on a pedestal—he can do no wrong. What happens when the boyfriend pressures her for sex? She gives in and compromises her morals and then could end up with a disease, pregnant, hurt emotionally, etc.*
- *She might feel totally rejected if the boyfriend breaks up with her. And because she believed he was perfect but doesn't want her, then she must be worthless…with a consequence of her self-hatred.*

So why is it bad to have an idol? It just means I feel bad after it hurts me, right? Or does it do more?

Desired Response: They may or may not have an answer but they should be thinking about it.

Here's a different question: Is a little bit of an idol enough? Does the amount you to pay to attention to that idol stay the same, get larger, or get smaller?

Desired Response: They hadn't really thought about it that way.

An idol is ultimately never satisfied. It's like the old potato chip ad on TV, "You can't eat just one!" Eventually a little bit of an idol isn't enough. It takes more and more attention, time, and (probably) money from us. And if you give it more and more, it could eventually kill you or destroy who you are by using you up. Draining your soul. If you keep giving it more of you, you'll even become like it, and that means you aren't you any longer. You are being destroyed.

> **POINT: The result of letting idols rule us is our own destruction. The idol will never be satisfied.**

TESTIMONY:

Arrange for someone to offer a brief testimony about idolizing an image.

Testimony Example: All my life I've looked at myself and felt that I just didn't measure up. I was small and skinny and had awful acne. Other popular guys were taller and had more muscles. I tried everything—diet supplements, body building, even steroids to buff up. I did get bigger, but all along I felt there was something they had that I lacked. That's driven me all my life, and it's led me to some pretty dangerous drugs. I understand now that God loves me as I am, and he's given me the body type I have. I now have the freedom to accept that about myself.

Why do we have these idols?

Desired Response: Probably no one will know, but maybe someone will say that it's because there are some unmet needs underneath.

What's under an idol is some unmet need that we have. Let's say that someone idolizes being thin. The deeper need might be to be attractive. Or it might be to live up to parental or peer pressures. Or even to be in control by not eating! What might the need be for someone who idolizes football or sports?

Desired Response: The need may be to be popular or important. It might be that the person needs to be somebody special because they don't feel good about themselves unless others pay attention.

The draw behind the attraction to an idol is that we think it will meet a need that we have. But ultimately we'll find that the idol is unattainable, and its demands can never be satisfied. When we continually focus on it, we get off track in our relationships, especially with God. Ultimately we need to look to God to meet our needs rather than to idols. We pursue idols because we think we'll be complete when we are like them or get them. We tend to think, "If only I had this, or if only I was that, then my life would be complete, and I'd have no problems." But only God meets our deepest needs for love, identity, and purpose.

POINT: Idols take the place of God in our lives as we attempt to meet needs in our ways instead of God's ways. It won't work.

My people have committed two sin: They have forsaken me, the spring of living water, and they have dug their own cisterns, broken cisterns that cannot hold water.
—Jeremiah 2:13

This verse gives us an image of what we run to. God is the true source, but we turn our backs. In turning our backs, we're tying to create a substitute for what we can only get from God. But our substitutes don't work.

God wants to meet our needs for love, for acceptance, for belonging, and for affirmation. Sometimes those needs are met as we come to him in prayer and pour our hearts out before him and listen to what he says or what we read in Scripture. Sometimes those needs are met through the people God puts in our lives who love, respect, and value us.

"LOVEFOOL"

THE POINT: Idols can be people from whom we try to acquire our identities.

SUMMARY: Participants listen to and discuss the lyrics to the song "Lovefool" by the Cardigans.

TIME NEEDED: 10 minutes.

MATERIALS: Boom box or sound system
"Lovefool" by the Cardigans (from the soundtrack for *Romeo and Juliet*—MP3s are readily available on the Internet if you'd rather not purchase the CD.)
Emotional Dependency by Lori Rentzel
Copies of lyrics to share with students (get them from the Internet)

CONTENT:

We're going to listen to a song. Check out the words and be thinking about what's going on in the song.

Stage: Play "Lovefool."

What was going on in the song?
Desired Response: The person idolizes her boyfriend so much that she'd be okay with him acting negatively toward her in just about any fashion.

Is that a healthy relationship? The lie is that romantic love can equal salvation.

Is it possible for a person to be an idol? To be too close to someone, to need them too much?
Desired Response: Yes.

What does that look like?
Desired Response: Clingy, the needy person wanting the idolized person to direct his life, the needy person can't make a decision without the idolized person, the needy person can't live without the idolized person.

Stage: If you can't get answers, prompt for idolatry in relationships. For example, "Do you think it's possible to idolize a person? What does that look like?" Then have two people act it out. Create variations of scenarios for them to improvise (e.g., "You believe you'll die without the other person. What might that look like?")

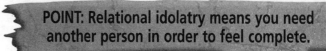
POINT: Relational idolatry means you need another person in order to feel complete.

There's a memorable line in *Jerry Maguire* where Jerry and Dorothy confess their love for each other. What is that all about? Is that true love or idolatry?

Desired Response: This should evoke some good discussion.

Yes, a husband and wife offer something to one another that they do not have alone. They complement each other. But if we can't also be okay with God alone—if that's, in fact, what God has in store for us—then we need to examine how much we're really allowing God to pursue us, shape us, relate to us, and fill us.

Relational idolatry means believing you need another person in order to be complete. One of the characteristics of emotional dependency is asking, telling, and demanding that someone else tell you who you are. But God wants us to depend on him and get our needs met through him.

What God wants for us, however, is to not look to a person or a relationship to tell us who we are or that we are worthwhile human beings. That way we can enjoy friendships without making excessive demands on others, expecting too much, or being devastated by them if they back away. We are secure in our identity because of our relationship with God.

Stage: Suggest that students read the booklet Emotional Dependency *if they want to understand this concept further.* (This small booklet is available from InterVarsity Press. It's a very quick read and really excellent material. Consider ordering some copies in advance if you think that you'll have students who are struggling with this issue.)

If you think you're in an emotionally idolatrous or emotionally dependent relationship, here are some good questions to ask yourself:

- Have you had sex with the person?
- Is the relationship closed and exclusive, or open and welcoming others?
- How well do you function without the person?
- Has the person become a greater focus than God?
- Has the person become your security and strength?

> POINT: We're set up for emotional dependency when there's something missing in our lives.

Why do we do it? Why do we become unhealthily dependent on people and relationships? Perhaps because there's something we're missing in ourselves. Maybe a past hurt has left us with a need inside we're trying to satisfy. Or maybe we just feel there's a big hole inside that we think we'll never fill. Maybe we have a need to be needed. Or we just don't feel adequate without someone else's reassurance and constant affirmation.

What Does a Healthy Friendship Look Like?

Lori Rentzel, author of *Emotional Dependency* (InterVarsity Press, 1984), compares healthy and unhealthy friendships.

A relationship is probably healthy if I:
- Free the other to have his or her own friends
- Include other friends in the relationship easily
- Allow the other to have independence and freedom
- Make my own plans and encourage the other to make their own plans
- Am aware of the other's good and bad traits and love the other anyway, encouraging the good
- Delight in the other finding new interests and friends and spending time with them.
- Enjoy their companionship when it's possible to be together

A relationship is probably unhealthy if I:
- Am possessive of the other or jealous of the other's relationships
- Want the relationship to be closed, isolated, or exclusive
- Am really angry or depressed if the other person withdraws slightly
- Am preoccupied with the other's appearance, personality, problems or interests.
- Am unwilling to make short or long-range plans that do not include the other person.
- Am unable to see the other's faults realistically
- Have to be with the other person all of the time.

TESTIMONY:

Arrange for someone to offer a brief testimony about emotional dependency.

Testimony Example: I was born three months premature, weighing about two pounds. I was kept in an incubator for two months, surrounded by caring nurses, but isolated and untouched by my mom and fed through tubes. What I didn't know until later was that the initial bonding so important for a baby never happened. I was left with a deep hole inside—always lonely, never getting the deep friendship or caring I needed. I always longed for deep friendship, especially with guys. I didn't realize that I wanted more of the only real affection I had known as a baby—the caring of my dad. That didn't seem to be a problem until I was married and realized that my needs were still there, and I was filling the holes in my life with other people.

POINT: You can't compromise with an idol. The only thing you can do is get rid of it.

"But what about an idol that's really something we need, like food or friendship? You can't stop eating forever and isolate yourself completely from everyone else, right?" Absolutely correct. In most cases, it's not the idol itself that's a problem—it's the worship of the idol. Food is necessary—but whether you're anorexic or overweight, food can become an unhealthy obsession that, when focused on, leaves no room for God to speak and act.

But the first step is this: Renounce your unhealthy worship of the object or person.

Here's what God says about idols:

"Teacher, which is the greatest commandment in the Law?" Jesus replied: "'Love the Lord your God with all your heart and with all your soul and with all your mind.' This is the first and greatest commandment. And the second is like it: 'Love your neighbor as yourself.' All the Law and the Prophets hang on these two commandments." (Matthew 22:36-40)

"You yourselves know how we lived in Egypt and how we passed through the countries on the way here. You saw among them their detestable images and idols of wood and stone, of silver and gold. Make sure there is no man or woman, clan or tribe among you today whose heart turns away from the LORD our God to go and worship the gods of those nations; make sure there is no root among you that produces such bitter poison." (Deuteronomy 29:16-18)

Wow, what strikes you about that verse?
Desired Response: Note that God's reason for not allowing idols is not so much his jealousy but because of the way they poison his people. God hates the results of idolatry in us.

"When the LORD your God brings you into the land you are entering to possess and drives out before you many nations... This is what you are to do to them: Break down their altars, smash their sacred stones, cut down their Asherah poles and burn their idols in the fire." (Deuteronomy 7: 1,5)

"Those who cling to worthless idols forfeit the grace that could be theirs." (Jonah 2:8)

"Dear children, keep away from anything that might take God's place in your hearts." (1 John 5:21, *The Living Bible*)

BREAKING IDOLS

THE POINT: We need to first identify the idols in our lives that Jesus wants to free us from, break their hold on us, and finally take the pieces to Jesus.

SUMMARY: Students decorate plaster "idols" to represent the things in their lives that they put before their relationship with God and break them.

TIME NEEDED: 15 minutes

MATERIALS: Inexpensive, four-inch terra cotta pots that you don't care about breaking
Colored markers
Tarps to cover floor (and later outside area) on which to make and break idols
Cassette or CD of appropriate songs for background music
Hammer or other tools to break idols
Cross to break idols in front of... or to place box of idol pieces in front of
Cardboard box to sweep idol pieces into
Broom to clean up

ROLES NEEDED: None

PREPARATION: None

The night of your meeting:
Lay tarps on the floor to protect it against the idol smashing—or find an outdoor location, like a parking area or deserted lot.

INTRODUCTION:

We all have idols in our lives. We're going to pray and ask God to show us if there are things in our lives that we've cared more about than him. Then we'll make our own idols for those things, renounce them, and break them.

Stage: Pray for God to show students what idols he wants to free them from…

Lord, come. Show us what we've put before you, the places where you want to break the power of idols in our lives. We want to renounce those idols and their power to identify us and hold us captive. But we can't do that in our own strength. So Father, come and pour out your love on us and show us what you want to free us from.

Now pay attention to what God brings to mind. Draw, write, or otherwise graphically symbolize that on your plaster idol. Let the idol represent the things you've worshiped other than God.

CONTENT:

Stage: Arrange idols and colored markers on tarp. Show an example—yours if possible—and explain what your idol represents. Let the group make their idols. You may want to play "music to break idols by"—either worship or mainstream music that reinforce breaking the power of idols in our lives. (Suggestions: "Lord of Every Man" by Craig Musseau, "No Other Gods" by Brian Doerksen, "Answer Us" by Andy Park, and "Arise Oh Lord" by Kelly Carpenter, all from Mercy Publishing.)

God wants to free us from the things that gotten in the way of our relationship with him. He knows that our idols will ultimately destroy us emotionally and spiritually…and he wants to break their power in our lives as we name them.

Stage: As an option, you may choose to send students to small groups before they break their idols. In groups they can share their idols and ask the group for specific prayer against the hold their idols have in their lives.

BREAKING IDOLS:

In the church we have sacraments—outward and visible signs of an inward and spiritual grace. In the sacrament of baptism, for example, we use water as an outward sign of the inward work God is doing in our hearts (dying to our sin and ourselves and being given new life in Christ). The church has used sacraments and symbols for centuries. Symbols matter. In fact, in some denominations, these are more than symbols—the sacraments connect us to a spiritual reality. Either way, God told us in the commandments not to make graven images—and not to have idols—for a reason. He knew it would be much too easy to worship things other than him. So…symbols represent a reality. What we're doing here is confessing with our hands and our artwork what we've done in our lives. So when we break these idols, we're doing something very important. We're showing God that we're ready to worship him alone and asking him to break the hold of these idols on our hearts. These symbols can have real power in our lives!

Stage: Pray together that God will honor our desire to put idols behind us. Idols and attachments should be renounced and their power broken in Jesus' name.

PRAYER BEFORE OR AFTER BREAKING IDOLS:

(Take a moment first to let students name their idols individually before God—silently or out loud.)

God we renounce these idols in our lives as we break the idols, we break their power over us and ask for your strength to be separated from these idols and to fill up the space they used to have in our lives.

Father, we break any ties with people or things that have been created because of these idols. We choose to look to YOU to meet our needs. Forgive us God for looking to other things or people to identify us—whether positively or negatively. Free us, Father, from the envy and control and jealousy we've held onto. And God, please come and show us how you really see us—and those people we've idolized. We choose now to let you be the one we desire—the only One who can meet our needs. In Jesus' name, amen.

Stage: Now for the idol breaking. Go to designated spots and give all students chances to break their idols, one at a time. Make this as solemn or as celebrative as you want: you set the tone. When the breaking is finished, put the pieces of the idols in a box and lay them before the cross.

Then pray for general closure for participants after idols are broken. If your group is open to sacramental expression, you may want to sprinkle or wash students' foreheads or hands with water to symbolize cleansing from sin as we were cleansed at baptism, or mark the forehead with oil to signify the presence of the Holy Spirit to fill the place where idols have been.

POSSIBLE SMALL GROUP QUESTIONS

SMALL GROUP GOALS:

- Name and renounce idols.
- Ask the Lord to meet our underlying needs.
- Ask God to fill the holes that are left after we have renounced our idols.
- Praying about the things that caused the idols to be there in the first place. (The needs…)

1. What have you identified as an idol in your life? Is it people, fantasies, situations, objects, or—?
2. What is the hardest idol for you to give up? Why?
3. Have people ever been idols to you? Did they know? If so, what was their reaction?
4. What idols does God want to free you from?
5. What's underneath that idol? What is it filling?
6. Does letting go of an idol make you excited or afraid?

INDIVIDUAL CHALLENGE AS A RESULT:

- I will renounce the people, things, or ideas that are my idols.
- I will put them out of my life.

RESOURCES AND REFERENCES

RELATED SCRIPTURES:

Exodus 20: 3-6 (The Ten Commandments)
Deuteronomy 7:1,5
Deuteronomy 29:16-18
Jeremiah 2:13
Jonah 2:8
Matthew 22:36-40
1 John 5:21

OUTSIDE REFERENCE MATERIALS:

Lori Rentzel, *Emotional Dependency* (InterVarsity Press, 1991). Excellent, short booklet describing what emotional dependency looks like, how it gets formed, and how to deal with it.

6

STICKS & STONES MAY BREAK MY BONES, BUT NAMES REALLY HURT ME

GOD'S OPINION OF YOU COUNTS MOST!

MAIN POINTS:

1. As God removes our layers of hurts and cleanses our sin, we're more able to see ourselves as we truly are.

2. We'll understand our identity as we become like Jesus and accept the changes he's causing in us.

3. When false labels are stuck on us, it's hard to believe the good that God says about us.

4. Our self-image is often far from the truth.

5. Developing a deeper relationship with God will move us closer to becoming who God wants us to be.

LESSON SEGMENTS:

Unveiling
True-False Labels
Self-Portraits

IN THIS LESSON...

Finding why God thinks you're so wonderful...

Finding the true you under
the layers of hurt and baggage...

UNVEILING

THE POINT: As God removes our layers of hurts and sin, we're able to see ourselves more clearly.

SUMMARY: To illustrate the point, a face familiar to the group is copied to an overhead and obscured with multiple layers of colored overhead transparencies. One by one the color transparencies are removed, and slowly the face becomes recognizable.

TIME NEEDED: 8 minutes

MATERIALS: Overhead projector
5 to 8 overhead transparencies to write on
Overhead transparency with a color photocopied on it. (You can take a blank transparency and any photo to a copy store and have it enlarged and color copied onto the transparency. Or you can scan a color photo into your computer and print it on a color transparency. (It's best if the photo is a candid or portrait of someone recognizable in class.)

PREPARATION: Before the meeting, ask a few students to color over the blank transparencies completely (like a 3-year-old might do)—as many transparencies as you have markers for. About 5 to 8 works well. (One color per page works well for the layering and unveiling process.) Collect those transparencies before the session starts.

When you're ready for the activity, lay the color photo transparency on the overhead and put the whole stack of scribbled transparencies on top of the photo, starting with the lightest colors and moving to the darker colors. When you finally turn the projector on, the photo will be obscured by the colored transparencies.

INTRODUCTION:

The process of becoming who God made us to be is a little like this:

Stage: Turn overhead on and show whole transparency stack, with the photo on bottom. You should only be able to see a well-lighted mess. Make sure the photo underneath is not clearly visible or identifiable. Ask someone to describe what they see on the screen.

Desired Response: A mess, color, scribbles—at most, a perceptive student may detect a photo at the bottom of it all.

Ever feel like that? A mess? I do! I feel like a complete scribble sometimes. What happens if I take a page or two away?

Stage: Remove one layer, then another, to show some change.

What do you see now?

Stage: Remove another layer or two—halfway there...

And now?

Stage: Continue sequence until you begin to see more and more of the actual photo. Notice and comment on that. Finish taking off layers so the whole group can see photo. Identify it.

Why did we do this? What can the layers represent?
Desired Response: Huh? No idea...

POINT: Healing is a process.

Let's let the layers represent what God is doing in our lives: taking off junk. It's a process...

Notice that the picture isn't perfect. Any picture—even a good one—won't be completely focused and clear when blown up and projected. On the contrary, it's grainy. Not crisp. It isn't perfect. But that's what God brought into being—and he's also pleased with who he created us to be.

POINT: We had to strip layers off the photos before we could see it clearly and with proper coloring. As God removes our layers of hurts and sin, we'll be able to see ourselves more clearly.

It's like when Lazarus was raised from the dead. Remember the story from John 11?

Stage: Someone probably knows the story...ask them to tell it. If no one knows it, you tell it.

Lazarus is sick, his sisters call Jesus for help, and Jesus WAITED for four days—and in the meantime Lazarus died. The family wasn't exactly pleased. Ever feel like that? You ask Jesus for help, but he seems to wait until you're dead to do anything, and by then it's too late? Well, THEN Jesus comes and proceeds to raise Lazarus from the dead. And he tells everybody to take the grave clothes off so he can go free. You see, Lazarus may have been revived, but he was still bound. And Jesus does that with us—he revives us AND removes our chains.

What are some of the things he takes off us? Sins we confess, masks and idols we leave at the cross, lack of forgiveness we lay down, addictions we ask him to break. Those are all layers. That's all the stuff covering up our pictures so we can't ourselves the way we really are.

The stuff we've been taking off—the stuff Jesus is removing and calling us out of—is what we'll call "the false self." It's all the self-doubt, the lies, the stuff we confess...and a lot more, as we'll see in a moment.

So what's left? The portrait! The person Jesus has made you to be. We'll call that the TRUE SELF. The person deep down at the center of who you are in Jesus.

TRUE AND FALSE LABELS

THE POINT: When we identify old labels, we can bring them to Jesus to take away or wash off. Then we listen for the names he has for us, and we use them to replace the old labels.

SUMMARY: Drawing and coloring the hurtful names and labels we've been called and listening for God's words about who we really are.

TIME NEEDED: 15 minutes

MATERIALS: Crayons, markers and paper—two sheets for each student.

INTRODUCTION:

Just as we often put labels on other people, we also live by the labels others slap on us. We receive our self-worth from their opinions. The taunts, criticisms, and sarcasm aimed at us can easily go all the way into us. What parents, teachers, or other authority figures say—even if it's not accurate—carries extra weight, and we can have a hard time believing that it may not be true.

And public ridicule or embarrassment creates an enormous amount of pain and makes us feel ashamed of who we are—not merely bad about things we may have done.

> **POINT: Labels that others have placed on us get in the way of our ability to see ourselves as God does.**

TESTIMONY:

Arrange for someone to offer a brief testimony about the effects of taunts or ridicule.

Testimony Example: I never seemed to fit in anywhere. And because the color of my skin was different, everyone—particularly in school—made sure I never fit in with them, either. Names like "blanket butt," "red skin," and "reservation trash." I had to change elementary schools three times due to all the harassment and taunting from schoolmates—and at one school, the principal even singled me out from all of my classmates for public punishment and humiliation. I really believed there was something inherently wrong with me. It was not until my mid-30s that I could take pride in my ethnicity (predominantly Latin American from South America) and know that there was never anything wrong with me at all. I was, and still am, fine the way God made me!

Take some paper and markers and crayons and anything else you'd like to write with—and write down the old labels, taunts, or criticisms that have gone all the way inside. Afterward we'll pray that Jesus begins to melt those labels, wash them away, and replace them with who he knows you really are!

Stage: Open the time by praying that God will bring to mind the old labels that He wants to deal with and to wash away. Then give the group 5 minutes to write down the labels they're hearing.

Now I'd like you to take the next 10 minutes and just be very quiet and listen for what God is saying to you instead of all those old words. It may be one word, a Scripture, or lots of things…a picture, a thought, a sense of calm.

Spend time in quiet and listen for what God is telling you. It may even seem like any old thought. But if it sounds good to you, it's probably God. Color as you think of new things. Draw your thoughts—or write them, or use a crayon and write a letter as if God was trying to communicate to you, or illustrate a Scripture the Holy Spirit is speaking to your heart.

So what is God saying in place of those false words?

Stage: Give the group some time to listen and write new words from God for them. You may want to provide some Scripture references and Bibles for kids to use. At the end, close with prayer.

WRAP-UP:

We need to accept our identity from God alone.

How? It's basically the process of becoming like Jesus.

So what can we do to help the process? Well, for all you active people who have a hard time just being and listening to God, here are some things you can DO:

1. Accept who he's making you to be.
2. Believe he's the one doing it and not you.
3. Continue with the process even when you're frustrated that you're "not finished yet." You will be! Don't beat yourself up; recognize that you're a work in process.
4. Listen to God (we'll talk more about this later).

SELF-PORTRAITS

THE POINT: There's a vast difference between the ways we see ourselves and the way God sees us.

SUMMARY: Participants compare self-portraits with actual photographs of themselves to demonstrate the vast difference between our perceptions of who we are and God's true perception of us.

TIME NEEDED: 20 minutes

MATERIALS: Handheld mirrors (one for each student)
Paper for each student
Markers or crayons
Instant camera
Film for camera (enough for one photo of each student)

INTRODUCTION:

Here's a chance for you to express your creative and artistic sides—even if you think you don't have one! You'll receive paper, markers/crayons, and mirrors. Use your mirror to take a good look at yourself, and then take about 5 minutes to draw a self-portrait.

Stage: While participants are drawing, go around the room and take a photo of each student to be used later in this lesson.

CONTENT:

Does anyone want to share what you've drawn?

Stage: Allow time for students to show off their work.

How close do these self-portraits represent what we really look like? They may reflect something about that person (great smile, blonde hair, pierced ears, etc.), but they aren't exact copies by any means.

Still, these pictures roughly represent how we see our exterior—but how do we feel about ourselves on the inside?

Stage: Allow time for response from participants if they are willing.

Here's the deal: We are NOT who others tell us we are—and neither are we what we often tell ourselves we are!

Stage: Ask a participant to read 1 Corinthians 13:12

"Now we see but a poor reflection as in a mirror; then we shall see face to face. Now I know in part; then I shall know fully, even as I am fully known." (1 Corinthians 13:12)

What is that Scripture revealing when it says "then we shall see face to face"? With whom will we be face to face?

Desired Response: God.

When we see God face to face, then we will know who we really are! Even a mirror can't give us an accurate picture of our true selves—the inside, where it counts! But God knows our innermost core.

Remember that who you really are is who God says you are, because he created you. He has known you from the very beginning! (Jeremiah 1:5)

CONCLUSION:

Now take a look at these…

Stage: Hand out photographs.

…and compare the photograph with your self-portrait. There's a little difference between them, huh? It's the same way with our self-image and God's image of us. And as much a difference that there is between our photos and our drawings, the way we see ourselves and the way God sees us is even more different. Vastly different!

God created you in love and adores you. In fact, you're his beloved.

Listen to this: God is always wanting to encourage and bless us. Hear the words of Zephaniah 3:17—*The Lord your God is with you. He is mighty to save. He will take great delight in you, he will quiet you with his love, he will rejoice over you with singing.*

Does that sound like the God you hear? He wants to sing over you. It's all about what we call GRACE…

We don't earn it, we don't strive for it, we don't get good grades for it, and we don't work toward it. God simply wants to give it.

For us God has love, care, intimacy, kindness, and words of love.

He wants us to climb up on his lap and listen and wait and know what he's really saying. He wants to find us!

How do we learn to see ourselves the way God sees us? Through relationship. Let's talk about our relationship to God, because that's the primary way we "get there." It's the primary way I become who God has made me to be.

> **POINT: There are five steps you can take toward becoming who God intends you to be.**

1. **Listen.**

   Life with God happens in conversation. All relationships are formed in conversation. But conversation is not conversation if it's all silence or all one-sided. LISTEN to God—he loves to pour out blessing and affirmation, not "shoulds" and commands. The Scriptures are full of God's communication to us.

2. **Spend time worshiping him.**

   Because we actually become like what we worship (just as people seem to resemble their dogs, or people's dogs resemble them, whatever…) And that's another good reason to break our idols.

3. **Get in his presence and let him wash off the old images of ourselves and the false labels we've believed.**

4. **Choose to believe the good things that God shares with you.**

5. **Really pursue God for his encouragement and blessing.**

   How do we pursue God? One way is to sit with him until he tells us who we really are.
   He wants to give us peace…
   He wants to comfort us…
   He wants to calm our fears…
   He wants to still the storm…
   He wants to give us courage and hope…
   He wants to put new names in our hearts…
   He wants to pour out the new words of blessing…

POSSIBLE SMALL GROUP QUESTIONS

SMALL GROUP GOALS:

- Become who God is making us to be through community.
- Let our small group act as community to reflect who we are becoming.

1. What are some of the "scribble" layers that cover who you really are?
2. We discussed our old images versus the how God sees us. What are some of your old images?
3. What old image is hardest for you to imagine getting rid of? Why?
4. What new images do you think God has for you?
5. Was it scary or encouraging hearing those things?
6. What are new images are hardest to believe? Why?
7. What positive influences are uncovering the "you" that Jesus is calling forth?
8. What old labels or new names would you like us to pray about for you?

INDIVIDUAL COMMITMENT:

- I will spend time with God, listen to him, and enjoy being with him.

RESOURCES AND REFERENCES

LEADER'S NOTES:

The following collection of verses could be printed and given to participants so they can explore scriptural principles upon which they can begin seeing themselves the way God sees them...

RELATED SCRIPTURES:

Deuteronomy 32:10-11
Psalm 17:8
Psalm 23:4
Psalm 139:14
Song of Songs 2:4
Isaiah 66:13
Zephaniah 3:17
Romans 1:7
Romans 8:1
1 Corinthians 13:12
2 Corinthians 1:3-5
2 Corinthians 3:18
Philippians 1:6
Colossians 3:12
1 Thessalonians 1:4

OUTSIDE REFERENCE MATERIALS:

Leanne Payne, *Restoring the Christian Soul: Overcoming Barriers to Completion in Christ through Healing Prayer* (Baker, 1996). Especially helpful is the chapter on Self-Acceptance.

Leanne Payne, *Listening Prayer: Learning to Hear God's Voice & Keep a Prayer Journal* (Baker Books, 1999). For those who want to really work further on listening to the affirming words from God.

INNOCENCE LOST

HEALING THE HURTS OF ABUSE FROM THE INSIDE OUT

MAIN POINTS:

1. Abuse is a misuse of power, violating personal boundaries.

2. We respond to abuse with self-protective reactions.

3. Our responsibility if we have been abused is ultimately to forgive—which is usually a process, not an event.

4. Jesus wants to set us free from the places of hiding and pain.

IN THIS LESSON...

Learn how to define abuse...

Find out what Jesus wants to do with your hurts and pain...

Begin the process of recovering from abuse...

LEADER'S NOTES:

Mandated Reporting: Abuse is extremely serious. There are serious moral and legal consequences not only for perpetrators but for you as a pastoral authority working with minors. You have a legal responsibility called "mandated reporting" whereby you must report suspected cases of abuse to authorities. Laws vary by state, so please find out the requirements in your state. Talk with your pastor in advance about how to handle any situations that might come up.

LESSON SEGMENTS:

The Plastic Wrap Wall
Heart Hurts

THE PLASTIC WRAP WALL

THE POINT: We react to the pain of abuse, often in hiding and building walls. Jesus wants to heal the pain and the wounds and protect us properly if we're willing to let him deal with the walls, heal our hearts, and ultimately if we're willing to forgive.

SUMMARY: A role-play demonstrates what happens when someone is abused. Characters act out the violation of the personal boundary we were born with; how we react and cope, and how we build walls to protect ourselves when we're abused; how Jesus enters and interacts in the scene… and how he redeems and heals us.

TIME NEEDED: 35 minutes **(Note: This is a long segment! You might need to limit sideline discussions from the sidebar materials but be sensitive to kids in your group for whom this is very close to home.)**

MATERIALS: Large cross approximately 5-feet high (or a student who will act as a cross—just make it clear somehow that the student is a cross, not Jesus hanging on the cross
Plastic wrap
Heart-shaped pillow (paper or cloth, stuffed) approximately 1-foot by 1-foot heart cover (fitted pillowcase or something that can cover the heart)
Washable black marker
2 chairs
2 rods to stretch plastic wrap between chairs that are positioned about four feet across from each other
Bed sheet with "SHAME" written in large letters (you can use the same bed sheet from the first session on Denial)
Bed sheet with scribbling all over it
Scissors
A foam or soft bat, stick (to hit with)
Cardboard boxes to build a wall (large enough to hide behind or within)
Approximately 20 sheets of paper and markers to label wall with

ROLES NEEDED: 4-5 volunteers, some will need to be prepped ahead of time

Victim (large role, always onstage) Should be prepped ahead of time. Try to have a good actor for this role—certainly someone who understands how it might feel to be abused. The best players for this role can act out how they've actually felt. The character should be reluctant at first to respond to Jesus and come out of hiding, but ultimately the victim is willing to allow God to work.

- Jesus
- Abuser
- Friend
- Person to mime being a cross as a new boundary, if a large cross is not available
- Rest of group to build plastic-wrap wall as boundary

PREPARATION: Copy roles for actors (pages 91-93)

Set up props for actors—

Jesus: gives heart to victim

Victim: has boxes, "shame" sheet, and scribbled sheet available

Abuser: has scissors, washable marker, and soft bat

Set up chairs and rods. (The rods should be situated vertically about 4 feet apart. Use tape to secure them to the chairs so they stand up.)

Have plastic wrap available, as well as markers, paper, and tape. Choose at least some roles in advance and prep actors.

INTRODUCTION:

We're going to discuss abuse. In this session we're talking about all-capital-letters ABUSE, not minor, lower-case abuse. We may or may not have been ABUSED, although we probably know people who have been—but we've all been hurt. So if you feel you can't relate to this topic, try thinking of times others have hurt you—I think you'll find the same principles apply.

What is abuse?

Desired Response: Most students will say, "Hurting someone." But if the response is this vague, push harder and probe for more specific answers that reflect the violence of abusive behavior.

Webster's definition of abuse:

To use wrongly or improperly misuse: to abuse one's authority. To treat in a harmful or injurious way: to abuse a horse; to abuse one's eyesight.

To speak insultingly or harshly to or about; revile.

To commit sexual assault upon.

Bad or improper treatment; maltreatment.

Rape or sexual assault.

This is our working definition: *Using power to hurt or destroy, breaking boundaries, and leaving destruction behind.*

This isn't a clinical or technical definition, but a working definition that allows us to discuss the issue.

POINT: Abuse means misusing power, violating boundaries.

Even sexual abuse is not about sex—it's about rage, violence, or power.

Abuse can be
EMOTIONAL
PHYSICAL
SEXUAL
SPIRITUAL
VERBAL

We're going to act out how abuse happens. To do this I need four volunteers. I need Jesus, a victim, a friend, and an abuser. Don't worry, no one will actually get hurt—and I'll talk you all the way through this, so you don't have to worry.

Stage: Pick parts and have those people come up front. It might help to have prepped some of the roles beforehand with team members in case there are no volunteers.

The rest of the group will be making a wall with this plastic wrap between these two chairs.

Stage: Stand the two rods vertically about 4 feet apart. Lean them against the chairs for support and them tape them to the chairs to secure them. Instruct participants to work with designated team member to build "wall" made of plastic wrap. The plastic wrap should be stretched between the two rod "end posts." While the plastic wrap wall is being built, prepare actors for their roles.

CONTENT:

Stage: Victim dances or moves or plays happily on one side of wall. Jesus is with the victim and gives the victim a heart. Victim may or may not know Jesus is the giver of the heart. Ask questions throughout sketch and direct it, telling players what to do and giving cues.

Describe the boundary or original wall.
Is it solid?
Desired Response: No, it's permeable—smells can get through plastic wrap in the fridge, etc. So can sound, light…

Can you see through it? Can someone get through or over it?
Desired response: Yes.

Let's see what happens when a friend comes along.

Stage: Cue friend to shake hands with victim over plastic wrap wall. Victim may or may not invite friend "in," and they hang out and talk, play sports, catch, whatever. Then friend leaves.

But is it still a good strong boundary?

Desired response: Yes.

What happens if someone forcibly breaks the boundary and does something to the victim? Let's watch and see...

Stage: Abuser pretends to be nice and helpful but also wants to cut the boundary. With or without permission, the abuser finally cuts the plastic wrap, comes in, and abuses the victim, beating him or her up. Writes with black ink on the heart with the washable marker. Abuser leaves. Victim hides hurt and starts to fiddle with heart while leader is talking. The victim eventually stuffs the heart in a box, sits on the box, and then puts together a wall using cardboard boxes to hide behind since boundary is broken.

Who could be an abuser?

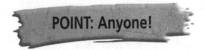

POINT: Anyone!

This includes siblings and peers—an abuser is often known by the victim.

What actions might constitute abuse?

Desired Response: Many...but make sure students include teasing.

In this sketch, did the victim deserve to be abused?

POINT: The victim never deserves abuse.

But an abuser almost always blames the victim and makes all sorts of statements designed to keep the victim subservient and powerless and quiet. The abuser tells the victim a lot of lies.

What kinds of things does the abuser say to the victim?

Desired Responses:
You deserve this.
You like this.
It's your fault.
Don't ever tell.
If you tell...no one will believe you.
It didn't happen.
I'm the only one who will ever love you.

What's the truth? Whose fault is it?

Desired Response: The responsibility lies with the abuser. Period.

Is there ever a scenario where the victim deserves abuse?

Desired Response: NO!

Stage: Victim hides behind the wall and throws the Shame sheet over the wall and himself or herself.

Now what's been happening to the victim?
Desired Response: Stuffed heart in box and sat on it...Built wall...Hid under dirty sheet and/or shame sheet.

What is in the box?
Desired Response: Heart.

What else is in the box?
Desired Response: The pain and the memory.

Where's Jesus?
Desired Response: Jesus is compassionate but outside the wall and the sheet.

What is the wall like compared to the original boundary?
Desired Response: Impossible to get through. Thick.

This wall is made of things we believe, and vows we make and statements we make as a result of the abuse (e.g., "No one will ever do this again.")

It's also made of results...
...For instance, a victim my turn to overeating to make himself bigger than his abuser...

What can one do in response to the abuse? What things might be written on the wall?

Stage: Pass out paper and markers and help participants think of things that are pieces of the wall—coping mechanisms, reactions, etc. Ask participants to write these down and tape them on the wall. Discuss as you go!

POSSIBLE RESPONSES:

Alcohol	Masturbation
Bullying	Plotting revenge
Clinging	Rebellion
Depression	Replacing abuser with someone else
Drugs	Self-hatred
Eating	Sex
Exploding	Suicidal self-destruction
Fear	Being the "tough guy"
Making oneself really ugly	

What's sinful in this situation?

Desired Response: What the abuser did, the stuff written on the wall, building the wall, hiding, etc.

Note that the abuse is not the victim's sin!

What does Jesus think about the abuse?

Desired Response: He hates it.

Where is Jesus?

Desired Response: He is nearby but not with victim—because of wall.

Where does the victim think Jesus is?

Desired Response: A long way away...

How does the victim feel? Does the victim want Jesus there?

Desired Response: The victim may feel the need to get cleaned up and make it all right before wanting Jesus.

The victim is under a sheet of shame that she thinks will hide her and keep us from seeing her or her stuff. But we see her anyway, don't we? And all it does is keep her from seeing all of us. Shame keeps Jesus—or anyone else—from getting in, and keeps an abused person imprisoned.

TESTIMONY:

Arrange for someone to offer a brief testimony about living with shame due to abuse for much of one's life, and how God is healing that.

Testimony Example: Shame always spoke to me in phrases: "If they knew you've been molested, what would they think? They'd be disgusted. No one will believe you. No one will love you. You're dirty. You're a freak. Don't ever let them know." All those phrases were lies. But why believe lies when I could have the truth? God's truth. So I'm learning to hear the truth about me—how God loves me and wants to heal me after what happened to me—instead of believing the self-condemning lies.

POINT: In order for a situation to change, Jesus has to enter the scene.

So what's next? How can this situation change?

Desired response: Jesus has to get close to the victim.

Stage: Jesus enters the picture—but only when victim is able to agree to his invitation of help or ask for help. The victim may say, "You can get rid of this sheet, but please don't take the wall down."

What does Jesus do first?

POINT: Jesus takes off the shame and puts it on the cross...

Stage: Jesus talks over the wall, asking if he can take the sheet off. After much fear and hesitancy and hemming and hawing, the victim finally agrees. Only then does Jesus take the shame sheet off and hang it on cross.

This is a hard step because it's often the shame that keeps us away from other people and Jesus.

Silence has been a big part of the abuse. The victim was probably told not to talk to anyone. Breaking silence—that is, telling others—may be a big part of breaking shame and the power of abuse.

Stage: Jesus asks if he can take down the wall—that is, remove the lies so the wall can come down. Victim is reluctant, but finally agrees. Jesus takes pages off wall and puts them on the cross. (Don't let this drag on…do it quickly.) Jesus begins to dismantle the wall, at least enough to reach the victim. Leave rest of wall for now.

> POINT: Jesus doesn't leave us defenseless. He doesn't rip off all our coping mechanisms at once or tear down the whole wall. He operates on what we can handle at that moment.

Stage: Jesus puts up a new boundary where old one was—using a large, portable cross (or a person to mime one).

Note that Jesus doesn't rebuild the old wall—he doesn't go back and make it like the incident never happened. But he cleans up the mess from the old boundary and puts a BETTER one there, since it is Jesus himself who stands in that very place now.

Stage: Cue Jesus to take care of the heart…
Jesus asks the victim for her heart, and the victim reluctantly agrees and hands Jesus the heart. Jesus takes the scribbled cover off the heart, uncovering the victim's pain of abuse. Victim cringes at discolored heart. Jesus puts the cover on the cross, too. He gives the clean heart back to victim.

> POINT: Jesus wants to heal our hearts and uncover them so he can ultimately restore them.

Note that the pain of the wounded heart has to go away. We can't hide in our pain. Some people get stuck in it, and then find they can't get out.

Forgiveness is the last step in the process—it takes down the rest of the wall. And we can't do it without Jesus' help. Then he can work on the rest of the wall.

> POINT: Jesus will help us to forgive.

Let's see whether our victim is able to forgive yet…

Stage: Jesus goes to victim and asks if she is willing or able to forgive yet…noting that it's her process and her forgiveness—but he'll make it possible. Victim may say yes or no. Either way Jesus encourages victim. If victim says yes, Jesus takes rest of wall down, hugs victim, and the scene is closed. If victim says no, Jesus hugs victim, and the scene is closed. Thank the actors, then wrap up.

WRAP-UP:

What's our responsibility when we've been abused?

> *Desired Response: To participate in our healing.*

Which means…

1. Talk
2. Invite Jesus in—he was always there anyway.
3. Be willing to face the pain with Jesus.
4. Take down the wall with him or let him do it.
5. Let Jesus place himself (symbolized with the cross) where the boundary was broken.
6. Forgive. (We'll talk about that in another lesson. For now, it's enough to know it's a process, not an event.)

Note that most of the process is Jesus' responsibility. We have to allow him to do his work!

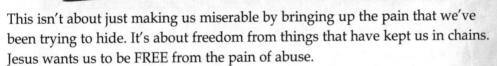

Point: Jesus wants us to be free—not hidden behind walls.

This isn't about just making us miserable by bringing up the pain that we've been trying to hide. It's about freedom from things that have kept us in chains. Jesus wants us to be FREE from the pain of abuse.

What hurts have beaten up your heart that Jesus wants to heal? What "lower-case" abuse has torn you down? What small hurts have made you build a wall? What big ABUSE has made you stuff your heart? Jesus wants you to be free from those hurts.

THE POINT: We want Jesus to identify and help us write down what places our hearts have been wounded by abuse. We want to identify where there are walls around our hearts and where he wants to come inside and heal.

SUMMARY: Red hearts are outlined on paper. Participants are asked to draw or write on the heart the things that have caused pain and have caused them to sin by hiding or by building walls around their hearts.

TIME NEEDED: 10 minutes

MATERIALS: Make enough copies of the heart on page 90 for all students. Markers/pens to write on hearts

PREPARATION: Photocopy heart outlines in advance and pass out to each student

INTRODUCTION:

There are lots of places where we've been hurt or ABUSED. Things happen every day that wound our hearts and make us want to hide.

CONTENT:

"Now the Lord is the Spirit, and where the Spirit of the Lord is, there is freedom." (2 Corinthians 3:17)

Jesus wants to free us from the stuff in our lives that makes us want to hide. Maybe he just wants to start the process and let us know it's safe enough to reveal the pain to him. Perhaps he's prepared to take off the shame or to begin removing parts of the wall.

What in your life does Jesus want to free you from? What hurts have sent you into hiding? Jesus wants to deal with those (he'll do it gently) and set you free. When he tells you what those things are, write them down on this heart.

Stage: Hold up red heart paper.

Let's ask him where we can start…

A leader should lead the group in prayer:
Holy Spirit, come and show how you want to make us safe enough to start this process. Show us, Lord, the things that have beaten up our hearts. Show us, Father, the places that we're hiding. We want to hear your voice, Lord, not the voices of the enemy, or of the lies we've believed, or of our fear or guilt or shame. We want to say "yes" to the places that you want to show us.

Encourage students to ask Jesus to come so he can make it safe for them to begin the process. He wants to impart the courage to start and the freedom of coming out from behind the wall!

POSSIBLE SMALL GROUP QUESTIONS

SMALL GROUP GOALS:
- Begin giving Jesus access to our hearts.
- Allow Jesus to open up a hole in our walls.

1. What is the state of your heart?

2. Where is it? In a box? Bruised? Broken?

3. What things have hurt your heart?

4. What things have you done in response to the hurt? Hide? "Stuff" your heart? Pretend that it didn't happen?

5. Can you imagine what Jesus might do with the pain and abuse you suffered? What is his reaction?

INDIVIDUAL COMMITMENT AS A RESULT:
- I will abandon the ways that I have coped by hiding my heart or blaming others or myself.
- I will allow Jesus to begin to touch the pain and the abuse and bring healing.

RESOURCES AND REFERENCES

RELATED SCRIPTURE:
2 Corinthians 3:17
Matthew 18:6-7

OUTSIDE REFERENCE MATERIALS:

Dan Allender, *Wounded Heart* (NavPress, 1990). For those dealing with significant abuse, this is a complete description of abuse and various reactions to being abused, the roles we learn to play as a result, and how to find healing. There's also a workbook to go along with the book that might be appropriate for individual follow-up if you have kids who've been abused.

Jan Frank, *A Door of Hope* (Here's Life Publishers, 1987). An incest survivor, Jan Frank describes common symptoms exhibited by abuse victims and a 10-step path to healing.

Leanne Payne, *Restoring the Christian Soul* (Crossway Books, 1991). Although not specifically on the topic of abuse, Leanne Payne outlines three key facets for healing—receiving love and acceptance, receiving forgiveness, and forgiving others.

David Seamands, *Healing for Damaged Emotions* (Victor Books, 1985). Another excellent resource for those with abuse backgrounds to come to terms with their personal histories and move beyond them.

ROLES FOR ABUSE INTERACTION:
"THE PLASTIC WRAP WALL"

VICTIM

You're onstage the whole time. If you're familiar with responding to abuse, feel free to add and improvise in this sketch. Leader will give you lots of clues as to what to do. You may play this by just responding to what's going on. Or you can follow these cues...

1. Interact with leader when appropriate—or when asked questions or when cued.

2. Start on one side of the plastic boundary. You are free, happy, playing, or dancing around. Jesus is there, too, but you may or may not see him. He gives you your heart, but you don't have to notice that it's him.

3. When a friend comes over, shake hands. Invite your friend into your side of the boundary if you want to. If you do, then have fun. BRIEFLY. Then your friend leaves.

4. When your abuser asks to come in, respond either yes or no. It doesn't matter, though, because the abuser cuts in anyway. You're scared and scream "no," but the abuser beats you up and takes your heart and scribbles on it.

5. You react by hiding and building a wall.

6. Start by stuffing your heart in a box TIGHTLY with all your pain and SIT ON THE BOX or hide it.

7. Then build a wall. Small at first, then really big. Finally, pull the dirty sheet over you, and then the shame sheet. (Or just the shame sheet).

8. Hide behind your wall.

9. When Jesus asks if he can remove the shame sheet, or the lies, or come in, readily agree to him getting rid of the shame and be reluctant about the rest. Improvise. Discuss with him, say no then yes (but don't take too long). If you want to hold on to certain lies and not let go of the papers, then tell him no. For example, when he wants to come in, perhaps you say no at first, then be fearful but let him in A LITTLE. He comes in somehow, gently, in a small space (ask him "Will it hurt?" and be really scared).

10. When Jesus is in, be scared to give him your scribbled heart but do it pretty soon (not immediately). Show that you are hurt when he opens the box because all the pain is in there, too.

11. When Jesus asks if you can forgive now, say whatever you want. Yes or no, either way he'll encourage you. Yes means he tears down the rest of the wall. No means he'll work on the process with you. At the end of the scene, whatever your decision, Jesus hugs you.

ROLES FOR ABUSE INTERACTION:
"THE PLASTIC WRAP WALL"

JESUS

You are present throughout the entire role-play, but have the most active role in the first and last scene.

1. In scene one: stand with Victim on same side of boundary.

2. You give Victim her/his heart. The two of you relate—but he or she may or may not recognize you gave him or her the heart. You stay fairly close to victim during the entire role-play.

3. Even when victim builds the wall to keep you out, stay right there on other side. Victim will not recognize you or let you in.

4. Pretend you're looking for ways to get behind the wall or get victim to see you (even saying "Remember me?" but victim doesn't see you).

5. When cued that it's time for shame sheet to come off, ask victim if it's okay. She or he may fight you or say no, but persevere, trying different ways until victim says yes. Take shame sheet off and put it on cross.

6. When cued that it's time to take down wall, take off lies (papers) first and discuss with victim how he or she can afford to get rid of this or that lie. For example, if page says "Overeating," you could say "Let's get rid of this one first—it's not healthy for you," etc. Victim will fight at first and then be willing.

7. When cued that it is time to tear down the wall, ask for ways to get in until they say yes. Create a tunnel, create a hole, find a way around, but DON'T tear down the whole wall. At least not at first.

8. Convince Victim gently that you will not hurt him. Reassure Victim. Tell Victim you love her and want to come nearer to help and to heal all the hurt. Eventually (perhaps sooner) Victim will let you in. Dismantle wall in whatever way you two have agreed on.

9. Make new boundary with the cross (or take person who mimes the cross to the torn plastic wall and have them be the new boundary). Tell Victim that this new boundary will keep her safe again so Victim doesn't have to use the wall anymore.

10. Go back to Victim and ask to see heart. Victim probably has it stuffed in a box. Tell victim you want to heal it. When Victim finally gives you the heart, show victim that you can give a new heart—take heart out of cover. **PUT DIRTY COVER ON CROSS.**

11. When cued regarding forgiveness, ask Victim if she can forgive now. Victim may say yes or no. Either way, encourage Victim in the process. If victim says "Yes," take down rest of wall and hug Victim. If not, just encourage Victim and say you'll work on the process together, and then hug Victim.

END OF SCENE!

ROLES FOR ABUSE INTERACTION:
"THE PLASTIC WRAP WALL"

FRIEND

You're in the second scene of the role-play: you are on the other side of the boundary from the victim. When cued, and as your youth leader is talking about the boundary—that is, the plastic wrap wall—then you go over and say hi to the victim. You reach over the boundary and shake hands. If invited (or if you want to) ask if you can go over and hang out with victim. Dance or play or laugh together. Improv as you wish, but then say you have to go, wave goodbye, and leave.

ABUSER

You're in the role-play's third scene. After friend visits Victim, you come over when cued. You are holding scissors, Nerf bat(s), and a washable marker. You can be either menacing or friendly. You ask Victim if you can come in. Victim may say yes or no, but it doesn't matter. You go in anyway.

Cut through boundary with scissors. Beat up Victim with soft bats (mime, don't hit hard, and let Victim mime being hurt). Take Victim's heart and scribble all over it with washable marker. Throw it back at Victim. Say some accusing line like, "Now you're no good for anyone!" or "Don't tell, it's our secret!" or "You know this is all your fault, don't you?" or some other lie.

Then go away.

PERSON WHO MIMES THE CROSS

Your youth leader will cue you to enter. You may be used in middle to end of role-play to drape shame sheet and papers on—but you will most likely just need to come in at end when Jesus puts a new boundary (that is, the cross—that's you) in place of the plastic-wrap wall. Pretend to be a cross and just stand there unless it becomes obvious that you could say something to help the interaction.

GRACE & LIBERATION

HOW FORGIVENESS SETS US FREE

MAIN POINTS:

1. When we hold back forgiveness, it's like a heavy weight we have to carry.

2. God doesn't view lack of forgiveness as healthy, and he warns strongly about its consequences.

3. Holding back forgiveness hurts us and doesn't accomplish what we want.

4. We believe lies about forgiveness (they're nothing more than myths). For example, we believe that forgiveness excuses sin, but it doesn't.

5. The reality of forgiveness is that it equals freedom.

6. We truly forgive when we forgive from the heart.

7. A change in perspective may make forgiving easier, but it's always a result of forgiveness.

8. There are steps toward forgiveness that can help us release our bitterness and know freedom.

9. We may need to forgive in order to have a peaceful, reconciled, and united community.

10. God wants to enable us to forgive.

LESSON SEGMENTS:

Rocks of Unforgiveness

Why Bother?

Thorns

Inductive Questions–
Forgiveness: Myth vs. Reality

Writing on Rocks

Painting Rocks Red

IN THIS LESSON...

We'll expose the myths about forgiveness...

Identify the burdens we carry when we don't forgive...

Take the first steps toward the freedom of forgiveness...

ROCKS OF UNFORGIVENESS

THE POINT: We carry around a heavy load when we hold back forgiveness.

SUMMARY: The rocks symbolize unforgiveness; in this lesson we'll carry
them around to symbolize the burden;
1. We write our unforgiveness on them
2. We paint them red to symbolize the blood of Jesus
3. Finally, we take them to the cross

TIME NEEDED: 5 minutes
Note: Rocks should be passed out to students several
hours/days in advance

MATERIALS: Overhead projector
Overhead transparencies
Overhead markers
Rocks—smooth enough to write on—one for each student

PREPARATION: Find a variety of rocks that could be comfortably carried
around in a pocket or even with two hands (though probably
not many of those!) Make sure the rocks are relatively clean. A
few hours or days before the lesson, ask students to take one
rock. After they have taken a rock, then tell them to carry it
around with them all of the time. All of the time means to
school...in the shower... to bed...etc. Don't tell them what the
rock signifies or why they're carrying it. That will be discussed
in the lesson.

INTRODUCTION:

Did you carry the rock around with you? Who remembered?

CONTENT:

How did it feel to carry the rock around all week?

Did you like it?

Did you want to get rid of it?

Did you make friends with it?

In this session, we're discussing forgiveness.
   Let's use this little or big rock as a symbol of unforgiveness. Sometimes, it's
just a relief to get rid of it. Sometimes we would rather be friends with it.
Sometimes even though the rock is a pain, we've gotten used to it.

What does unforgiveness look like? Let's say you're mad at someone—so what do you do or think or feel when you do not want to forgive them?

Stage: Write answers on overhead. Look for answers like getting revenge or hurting them back.

Why are you doing this to them? Just to be nasty? Or is there more reason?
Desired Response: To protect yourself... because it hurt... because they deserve it... etc.

How well does it work? Does it do a good job of protecting or of getting revenge?

WRAP-UP:

> **POINT: When we carry unforgiveness, it's a heavy burden.**

Unforgiveness may become a burden, or it may be something we're comfortable with. But it's not good for us—and it doesn't really protect us, either. We'll come back to what we'll do with our rock in a few minutes.

LEADER'S NOTES:

You may find that some kids will hate their rocks for the inconvenience and others will make friends with them. Maybe one kid gave the rock a name and dressed it up! Use their responses to their rocks creatively as you teach. For example, some students make friends with their unforgiveness and grudges even though it's counter-productive in the long run.

WHY BOTHER?

THE POINT: God believes unforgiveness is unhealthy. He warns strongly about its consequences.

SUMMARY: The group acts out the parable of the unmerciful servant and then discusses what it means. We recognize that God hates unforgiveness and deals harshly with it; we discuss how to reconcile that with our concept of a merciful God who isn't angry. We discuss myths about forgiveness and who it hurts, etc.

TIME NEEDED: 10 minutes

MATERIALS: None

ROLES NEEDED: Director
Narrator
Jailer
Servant who owes master millions of dollars
Another servant who owes first servant a few cents
Master
Other servants who are displeased

INTRODUCTION:

Let's see what the Bible says about unforgiveness.

Stage: Read the story of the unmerciful servant, Matthew 18:23-35

Time for an improv! I will slowly read the text of the story, and the characters will act it out as they hear it read. Who's willing to volunteer for this sketch?

Stage: Assign roles and begin the improv skit. As you read, leave pauses for students to elaborate the action or improve lines of dialogue.

CONTENT:

What does the story have to say about unforgiveness?
Desired Response: It's wrong, it hurts us, God doesn't like it, etc.

What are we supposed to forgive?
Desired Response: Everything.

How does God feel about unforgiveness?
Desired Response: He feels strongly about it. He punishes it. He wants to change it, etc.

But I thought Jesus was always forgiving. You mean he's not? He gets mad when we do not forgive?
Desired Response: Anything! Have a discussion about different aspects of God's character or just make the point that God's not out to punish us. Continue discussion as long as you wish.

 POINT: God knows lack of forgiveness isn't healthy, and he warns strongly about its consequences.

What about the place in the story where the man is thrown in prison—does it mean that God gets angry and throws us in prison when we don't forgive?

Stage: Solicit various responses—and if they're stuck, go to the next question about what else the prison could represent.

So what else could the prison represent?
Desired Response: The stuff we feel when we don't forgive; the consequences of our unforgivenesss.

Unforgiveness...
...keeps us attached to the person we're mad at—in our hatred we focus on them.
...comes between us and God. (Matthew 6:14)
...doesn't allow the situation to get better or change.
...prevents dialogue.

Matthew 6:14 says, *"For if you forgive men when they sin against you, your heavenly Father will also forgive you. But if you do not forgive men their sins, your Father will not forgive your sins."*

So let's review: Why should we forgive?

1) God has commanded us to. (Matthew 6:12)
2) Relationships and forgiveness are important to God. (Matthew 18:23-35)
3) Jesus has forgiven us. (Colossians 3:13)
4) Relationships are more important to God than the religious stuff we do! (Matthew 5:24)

WRAP-UP:

We talked about some of what we feel when we don't want to forgive. The stuff that happens to us when we don't forgive isn't very fun. Let's look at some of it.

THORNS

THE POINT: Holding onto unforgiveness hurts us and doesn't foster what we really want (which is safety and protection).

SUMMARY: We illustrate the "thorny" relationship and problem by using a rose, holding it tightly. We injure ourselves by holding tightly and not forgiving, and we find ourselves hurt by the very thing that we thought would protect us.

TIME NEEDED: 5 minutes

MATERIALS: Vase filled with water
One long-stemmed rose with thorns, set in the vase
One thick garden glove

ROLES NEEDED: None

PREPARATION: Put water in vase and set rose in vase. Have glove ready to put on—or put it on just before the illustration.

INTRODUCTION:

POINT: When we hold onto unforgiveness, the relationship with the other person can get thorny. We think perhaps we're protecting ourselves or hurting the other, but in reality we hurt ourselves.

CONTENT:

Stage: Refer to rose in vase.

It's as if my feelings about the person I'm not forgiving are this rose. It's a beautiful flower, but it has thorns. I can look at it and love it and smell it and agree intellectually that it's beautiful.

Stage: Pick up rose in hand without glove to illustrate point.

I can even take it from the vase and hold it. But if I'm wounded by the thorns, that's a problem. Even then, if I hold it lightly, I can hold the rose by the stem without hurting myself.

Stage: Change to gloved hand and start to hold tighter and tighter.

But if I hold the rose very tightly by the stem with the thorns, and I think, "I'm going to hurt this person by holding on to the unforgiveness and crushing them hard with it 'cause they really REALLY deserve it!"...or I think, "I hope it hurts them as much as it hurt me!" or "They don't deserve forgiveness" or "This will keep me from getting hurt by them again!" then guess what I'd do to my hand? I would tear it up with the thorns. In order to even show you what I mean I have to use this glove.

> **POINT: The harder I hold on to the unforgiveness to protect myself, the more it may hurt me!**

Stage: Change back to other hand, hold rose loosely.

If I forgive, I can release the person and see the rose for what it is—and without being skewered by the thorns. And any hurts I've suffered from the thorns can heal as well.

Stage: Put rose back in vase.

And I can even begin to see this as a rose again—something really beautiful—and not focus on the pain of the thorns.

WRAP-UP:

It's the same way with people—they have thorns, and occasionally we get stuck by those thorns, or even torn up pretty badly. But as we forgive, we can see them the way they really are—thorns and all—and not get hurt by them.

Here are some of the ways that holding on to unforgiveness hurts us (and not the people we're holding grudges against):

- We stay overly sensitive to the person and get hurt again easily.
- We get absorbed protecting ourselves or justifying ourselves.
- The person we're angry at "moves into our heads"—every thought of the person stirs up pain again.
- By letting them into our heads, we give them way too much control of how we feel.

FORGIVENESS: MYTH VS. REALITY

LEADER'S NOTES:

A common question is whether forgiveness equals a fully restored relationship. Is forgiving the same as being reconciled? Not at all! Forgiveness is different than trust. Even Jesus said he trusted himself to no man because he knew what's in the hearts of men (John 2:24-25). But he loved unconditionally and forgave constantly. Romans 12:18 says, "If it is possible, as far as it depends on you, live at peace with everyone." The reality is that relationships are two-sided. We may do everything possible on one side and not be able have a relationship if the other side just doesn't want it.

It's also possible to stay in relationship with someone who has hurt us as long as different boundaries are set-so that what hurt us in the past won't continue in the future.

If we forgive in a relationship, our vision gets clearer so we can see the other person realistically-and learn how to develop HEALTHY relationships with them.

THE POINT: We know a lot about forgiveness, but we may not know what it isn't. We believe lies that keep us from forgiving.

SUMMARY: Participants are asked to list and explore the myths we've believed about forgiveness—and what forgiveness really means. Myths that we discuss include "forgiveness equals excusing sin" and "forgiveness means it will happen again."

TIME NEEDED: 15 minutes (make copies of page 108 first)

MATERIALS: Overheads and marking pens to record responses from participants

INTRODUCTION:

We've looked at unforgiveness—now let's look at forgiveness.

CONTENT:

First of all, instead of defining what forgiveness is, let's look at what we believe about forgiveness.

> **POINT: There are lots of myths we believe about forgiveness.**

What are some things that keep you from forgiving-things you believe about forgiveness?

Desired Response: Solicit responses from participants. You may include these:

 Forgiving is saying it's okay for the other person to hurt me again

Forgiving means "They" will take advantage of the situation and do it again (not return money, for example)

Forgiving means I have to forget the situation

Forgiving means no justice will be done

Forgiving means there's no vengeance

Not forgiving means I'm hurting the other person

Forgiving leaves me emotionally naked and unprotected

Forgiving means I will be weak and they will be strong

Forgiving makes the sin okay

Forgiving means just pretending that everything's fine, even if I still hurt

Forgiving is just words

Forgiving means I have to trust the person as though it never happened

What is the reality instead of the myth? What is forgiveness?

Desired Response: Solicit responses from participants. You may include these:

- Forgiveness means I'm not going to take revenge. (It's God's place to take revenge.) *Romans 12:19*

- Forgiveness acknowledges the depth and reality of the wound.

- We may get hurt again, but we can see clearly to have a right view of that situation, not replaying the old situation or seeing the new situation with old lenses.

- Forgiveness means letting go of what hurt us or what happened.

- Forgiveness doesn't mean putting our pearls before swine (Matthew 7:6) or laying our hearts on the line to be abused again.

- Forgiveness doesn't mean excusing sin and saying it didn't happen—forgiveness means letting go of the resulting hurt.

- Forgiveness doesn't mean we have to forget.

- If we forgive once, it's easier to forgive the next time.

- If we practice forgiving little things, it's easier to forgive the big hurts when they happen.

- Forgiveness frees us to see relationships rightly and not be fearful or overprotected.

- Forgiveness keeps us right with God.

- Forgiveness lets God be the judge.

- Forgiveness helps us heal.

- Forgiveness is a process—it takes time.

- Forgiveness requires God's help—he empowers us to forgive.

- The hurt has to go somewhere—to Jesus, on the cross-not staying lodged in our hearts.

- Forgiveness is the best thing for us!

- Forgiveness is a choice we may make—and it can be hard.

- Forgiveness is a gift freely given.

- Forgiveness is an affront to our sense of justice—we believe the person who hurt us doesn't deserve forgiveness.

- Forgiveness is a discipline that makes us more like Jesus.

Why don't we forgive?

Desired Response: Because we're afraid, or still believe the myths, or because we're still in the process.

How quickly does forgiveness happen?

Desired Response: Sometimes it's a process—it can take a long time. Sometimes it takes a second.

LEADER'S NOTES:

Scientific studies show that forgiveness is a key to overcoming depression, heart disease, and other disorders. (Arnold, *Seventy Times Seven Workbook*, pg. 7) Two big reasons why Christians have emotional problems are, first, a failure to receive and live out God's unconditional grace and forgiveness and, second, an unwillingness to offer that love, grace, and forgiveness to others. We read and speak about God's grace, but we don't let it touch the level of our emotions. (David Seamands quoted in Phillip Yancey's *What's So Amazing About Grace?* pg. 14)

POINT: Forgiveness is a process. That means that you forgive as much as you are able now... and you may have to go back and forgive more later.

For example, you may be beginning a process, just realizing something really happened and you need to forgive that hurt. Or you may be in the end of a process, and all that needs to happen is prayer or having others pray with you. Or you may be in the I'm-not-willing-Lord-but-I'm-willing-for-you-to-make-me-willing place.

> *Stage: Pass out the repro page,* The Parable of the Unmerciful Servant *(page 108).*

Could I have a few volunteers read the parable?

In the parable it talks about forgiving your brother from your heart. What do you think that means? What steps might you have to go through to really forgive from the heart?
> *Desired Response: Releasing feelings, understanding the other perspective, receiving healing, etc.*

It is important to forgive but from the heart. You have to work through the feelings. But failure to forgive at all is not an option. True forgiveness means one has to decide from the heart!

POINT: Actually, it's God who gives us the ability to forgive! He's willing to do the hard work.

If you choose to say, "God I want to be able to forgive," God will make it happen.

What happens when we forgive?
> *Desired Response: It frees us; it releases the other person from our bad feelings.*

Who might it help when we forgive? Us? The other person? Is it easy?

TESTIMONY:
Arrange for someone to offer a brief testimony about the difficulty of forgiveness—and how it was realized.

> *Testimony Example: Forgiveness seemed impossible for me. Holding my anger always felt like a protective barrier between me and anyone who hurt me so I wouldn't be hurt again. But God asked me to forgive a friend who hurt me badly. And when I was able to hand over my bitterness to Jesus, I felt like a cinderblock was lifted off my shoulders! I never trusted her like I did before, but I forgave her and it has set me free.*

POINT: Forgiveness always sets us free. It always has benefits.

LEADER'S NOTES:

It's not necessary (and usually not appropriate) to tell the people we've forgiven that we actually have forgiven them. It is appropriate, however, to ask forgiveness for any ways you've wounded them through responding to them in anger, hatred, bad-mouthing, etc. But it's totally appropriate to confront others about things they've done to you! (i.e., Give them a chance to ask for forgiveness.)

Encourage students to work through forgiveness for the person first before confronting a person so that the past doesn't get in the way of relating to him/her or create worse interpersonal conflict.

WRITING ON ROCKS

THE POINT: Forgiveness relieves us of heavy burdens; God wants to enable us to forgive, or at least begin to participate in that process.

SUMMARY: Students write names, events, or symbols on rocks to represent the people and events we are giving over to God, either forgiving or beginning the process of forgiveness.

TIME NEEDED: 10 minutes

MATERIALS: Rocks that students carried around before; permanent markers

PREPARATION: Pass out markers to students

INTRODUCTION:

We've carried our rocks around long enough. It's time to name them and stop carrying the burden around.

CONTENT:

What people or situations do you think God want you to forgive right now? Perhaps a friend, or a family member, or God, or ourselves. Maybe there's a small, easy one...and maybe there's one a lot bigger than that.

We're going to pray because there may be lots of people or events we need to forgive. But there may be only one or two or three that God wants to help you with RIGHT NOW. Some of us are at the very beginning of the process and only able to say, "God, I don't know about this, but I'm willing." Wherever we are in the process, we're going to write those one or two or three people or situations on those rocks we carried around.

PRAYER:

Holy Spirit, come. Create here a safe place so we can begin to deal with forgiveness. And Lord, we want to hear only YOUR voice, not our voices of shame and guilt and "should haves." Keep us from doing this on our own strength, Lord. We only want to deal with the hurts on your agenda. Give us hearts, Lord, that desire freedom from the bitterness, hatred, and resentment that hold us captive. Father, who are you bringing to mind for me to forgive? We're tired of carrying around heavy rocks of unforgiveness. Come and show us, Lord, where we are in the process. What people or events do you want to enable us to forgive?

   Stage: Wait in silence for a few minutes.

In this process, if you aren't ready to begin it yet, that's okay. Give that to God, too! That way he can help you wherever you are. He knows it's tough, and if you're having trouble, he's not angry. He understands why you're having trouble.

Stage: Wait in silence for a few more minutes.

Now if a name or two or three—or an event or two or three—came to mind, write them down on the rock. Later we will pray over the rocks and take them outside and paint them red—and put them in front of the cross.

Forgiveness is a work of grace that happens on God's timing. Be aware that it's possible to try to force yourself to forgive too soon—usually before the depth of the hurt is fully realized. That's okay, but you find yourself needing to repeat the forgiveness process later.

PAINTING ROCKS RED

THE POINT: Jesus forgives all the things we bring to him and enables us to forgive the most painful places of our lives. There isn't anything he doesn't want to take and redeem.

SUMMARY: We pray about the hurts written on the rocks and then paint the rocks red to symbolize the blood of Jesus covering those things. Finally we put the rocks in front of the cross as an act of worship.

TIME NEEDED: 10 minutes

MATERIALS: Tarp or large sheets of butcher paper to protect ground or floor from paint
Rocks or heavy objects to hold tarp/paper down (especially in inclement or breezy weather)
Newspaper to place rocks on when placing them in front of cross
Box big enough to place rocks inside and spray paint them
Disposable vinyl or latex gloves
Red spray paint
Rags and paint thinner, if needed for cleanup

ROLES NEEDED: Someone to lead worship after rocks are placed at the foot of the cross

PREPARATION: Set up tarp and paint before going outside—or have someone do it during earlier during this lesson
Use rocks to hold tarp in place
Put newspaper over tarp and box (in which to paint rocks) on top of tarp
Put newspaper in front of cross
Have box or newspaper available to carry rocks to cross
Have disposable gloves ready so participants can avoid getting too messy
Make copies of pages 109-110

INTRODUCTION:

We've written on our rocks the hurts and pain we're giving to God. Now we're going to paint those rocks red—a symbol of Jesus' blood. In Ephesians, Paul tells us, "God is so rich in kindness that he purchased our freedom through the blood of his son, and our sins are forgiven." (Ephesians 1:7, *The Message* translation)

When Jesus died, all the bad stuff we've done was heaped on his shoulders —along with all the stuff that's been done to you and the pain it caused.

Now, by giving Jesus the red rocks, we're reminding ourselves that there isn't anything that his death wasn't good enough to take care of. He died so that we could be forgiven for harboring bitterness and resentment toward people who've hurt us—and so we could be healed from the wounds others have inflicted on us. Whether it's our unforgiveness or the worst sin in the world that someone did to us, it doesn't matter—Jesus took care of it.

When we're forgiving horrible hurts done to us, we're saying "Okay God, I'll let you take care of making it right instead of me." And the red paint symbolizes that Jesus has already taken care of that by dying.

POINT: God has taken care of it by pouring out his blood.

In a minute we're going to go outside and paint these rocks red. Then we'll come back in and place them at the cross and leave them there. That will symbolize the fact that we don't have to keep carrying our burdens and hurts and pain.

But first, let's pray.

(It's okay to tell the Lord silently how you feel as a result of the pain and hurt of those people and situations. As God gives you grace, do what he's shown you. Hand him each of the situations and names on the rock. See what he does with those...)

PRAYER:

Lord, I want to give to you this rock, and the names and all the things it represents. Father, I'm willing to release these people and events to you, and I ask right now for the grace and the gift to be able to forgive these people and events and let you take them.

Lord, I choose to forgive the people and situations on this rock. I choose to let them go and let you take care of the results.

Stage: Wait and let people do that...

Father, some of these events are still incredibly hurtful. I pray you would be very close as I release to you the people and the pain that I've carried for this long time.

And Lord, please come and be the protection I need so that this situation will not happen again or hurt me again. Show me, Father, how you're standing between me and the situation or the person and creating a new boundary.

Wherever I am in the process, Lord, I give you both the rock and the result. And Lord, I ask you to come and bring blessing out of the pain of the things that happened, and that you would redeem them.

In Jesus' name, Amen.

Stage: Hand out the Steps of Forgiveness *repro sheets (page 109-110) for kids to have a written outline.*

Now some of you may need to go further than that, and actually go through each of the steps in the forgiveness process. If you do, then please, find someone to do that with—or do it specifically in your small group. It really takes care of a lot! But wherever you are in that process, we're going to paint the rocks red right now, and then put them in front of the cross.

Stage: Paint rocks outside in a place where the paint won't stain anything or use a box that's big enough so you can place the rocks inside and paint them.
Be sure the place you use is well protected and well ventilated if it's not outside.

God is very excited to see people forgive, because he knows it'll set them free. He wants to release you from all the hurts and pain that have held you back and kept you from being closer to him and more able to do all the good things he has prepared for you to do!

Stage: When people are finished painting rocks and the rocks are dry enough to move (on paper), place them in front of the cross as an act of worship. "At the Cross" is a wonderful worship song to accompany this exercise. If it wasn't done during small groups, volunteers may wish to pray for students individually during this worship time, declaring the forgiveness of the Lord for anything that's been confessed, and asking the Holy Spirit to come and fill all the places where the pain and unforgiveness have been.

POSSIBLE SMALL GROUP QUESTIONS

SMALL GROUP GOALS:

➤ Enable participants to forgive.

1. Did the Lord bring to mind people he wants to help you forgive?
2. What did you write on your rock?
3. What have you seen in your own life that has resulted from lack of forgiveness?
4. What areas of your life are tough for you because you have walled yourself off?
5. How does it feel to write something on the rock?
6. Is there someone who needs prayer from the group in order to help them to forgive?

INDIVIDUAL CHALLENGE AS A RESULT:

➤ I will choose to forgive _____ and release that person to the Lord.
➤ I will allow God to begin the process of forgiveness in my heart.

RESOURCES AND REFERENCES

RELATED SCRIPTURES:

Matthew 18:23-35
Matthew 5:23-24
Matthew 6:12, 14-15
Matthew 7:6
Colossians 3:13
Ephesians 1:7
John 2:24-25

OUTSIDE REFERENCE MATERIALS:

Dan Allender, *Bold Love* (Navpress, 1993).
Excellent treatment of the difference between forgiveness and reconciliation.

Paul Meier, *Don't Let the Jerks Get the Best of You* (Thomas Nelson, Nashville, 1995).

Lewis Smedes, *Forgive and Forget: Healing the Hurts We Don't Deserve* (Harper, San Francisco, 1996).

PARABLE OF THE UNMERCIFUL SERVANT

MATTHEW 18:23-35

"Therefore, the kingdom of heaven is like a king who wanted to settle accounts with his servants. As he began the settlement, a man who owed him ten thousand talents [Editor's Note: A few million dollars!] was brought to him. Since he was not able to pay, the master ordered that he and his wife and his children and all that he had be sold to repay the debt.

"The servant fell on his knees before him. 'Be patient with me,' he begged, 'and I will pay back everything.' The servant's master took pity on him, canceled the debt, and let him go.

"But when that servant went out, he found one of his fellow servants who owed him a hundred denarii [editor's note: a few dollars]. He grabbed him and began to choke him. 'Pay back what you owe me!' he demanded.

"His fellow servant fell to his knees and begged him, 'Be patient with me, and I will pay you back.'

But he refused. Instead, he went off and had the man thrown into prison until he could pay the debt. When the other servants saw what had happened, they were greatly distressed and went and told their master everything that had happened.

"Then the master called the servant in. 'You wicked servant,' he said, 'I canceled all that debt of yours because you begged me to. Shouldn't you have had mercy on your fellow servant just as I had on you?' In anger his master turned him over to the jailers to be tortured, until he should pay back all he owed.

"This is how my heavenly Father will treat each of you unless you forgive your brother from your heart."

STEPS OF FORGIVENESS

1. We all cover our pain with coping mechanisms that sometimes mask the underlying issues. Ask God to show you what's at the root of your pain, where we have been hurt and by whom. If your coping mechanisms are sinful—such as drinking to kill the pain or violent outbursts—then confess those as sin and ask God to forgive you.

2. Pour out your heart to God about your feelings toward the person you're holding a grudge against. It's helpful to speak to the person as though the person were present. Say everything you need to and don't try to control emotions that may rise up during this time. This is a form of confession. You may be surprised to find attitudes you weren't consciously aware of surfacing. Some of these you may need to confess as sin as well.

3. By a choice of your will, choose to forgive the person specifically for each attitude, word, or action that has hurt you. Speak as though the person were present in the room, right next to you. For example: "Dad, I choose to forgive you for the time you made fun of me in front of my friends at the school play." Then ask God to forgive the person specifically for the hurt done to you. Again, speaking it out loud really helps.

4. Release God from any of unforgiveness or anger you're holding toward him for letting it happen, confessing it as sin. Recognize that God was present to the situation and as heartbroken as you were.

5. Ask God to forgive you for any bitterness, unforgiveness, resentment, hatred, avoidance, revenge, or blaming.

6. Renounce and break any judgments you may have made against the person.

7. Invite the Spirit of God to come and heal those areas of your heart and memories that have been bound by hurt and unforgiveness. The healing here often comes with emotional release and the Spirit often shows us how God saw the original situation. Expect God to reveal himself to your past in prayer.

8. Invite the Lord to fill your needs so you'll stop looking to others to meet needs that should be met in God.

9. Ask God to fully bless the person who has hurt you. If you have trouble doing this, ask God to show you more about the situation and work through any additional unresolved areas.

FINALLY...

Take time to deal with this before God. It's not just a rote exercise. Finding another person to help facilitate the confessions and to pray for you during this process is really helpful.

And even if you don't fully get in touch with deep feelings, you can still move through the steps. If later it seems the process was incomplete in any way, God is faithful and you can walk through the process again as God gives more insight. Forgiveness can be repeated like peeling off the layers of an onion.

If you get "stuck" in the process, consider why you are stuck at that particular point and seek the Lord. It may be that God wants to reveal more about you, the other person, or the situation before you are ready to move on.

HOOK, LINE, & SINKER

RESISTING TEMPTATION AND BREAKING ADDICTIONS

MAIN POINTS:

1. Temptation is not a sin.

2. When we are presented with a temptation, we can find a way out.

   - We can flee from temptation.

   - We can focus on Jesus.

   - We can find accountability and support.

3. We balance pain with pleasure. When we are hit with pain, we feel a need for pleasure to offset the pain.

4. Addiction is when we are compulsive about behavior and cannot break free.

5. Addictions develop into cyclical patterns that reinforce the acting out behavior.

IN THIS LESSON...

Learning how to face temptation without falling into sin...

Receiving God's strength to resist the things that tempt you...

Learning about the pattern of addiction and how to break the cycle...

LESSON SEGMENTS:

Run, Joseph, Run!
Finding a Focus
The Pain/Pleasure Balance
The Cycle of Addiction

RUN, JOSEPH, RUN!

THE POINT: When presented with temptation, we mustn't simply dwell on fighting it. Rather, we must take action and flee.

SUMMARY: Students review the story of Joseph and the temptation he faced with Potiphar's wife.

TIME NEEDED: 10 minutes

MATERIALS: Bibles or printout of Genesis 39:7-23 (the story of Joseph and Potiphar's wife)

LEADER'S NOTES:

You may want to divide this session in two by emphasizing temptation first and addiction second. That would give adequate time for more discussion or to dive somewhat deeper. If you do so, you may want to have the group act out the forthcoming story about Joseph and Potiphar's wife. Appoint someone as the "director" and let that student figure out how to stage it. Leave no more than 10 minutes to prepare. It's lots of fun!

INTRODUCTION:

Any struggle with sexual or relational brokenness involves a struggle with temptation. Whatever we're tempted with leaps off billboards, corners, conversations, TV shows, and relationships. If I have a weakness for blonde hair and blue eyes, that's what I'll see. If I have a weakness for fixing people's problems, they will all come to me. Imagine for a moment that you are being tempted...

How do you feel when you are tempted?
   Desired Response: Guilty, frustrated, angry, weak, self-doubting.

The apostle Paul knows all about being tempted:
"I know that nothing good lives in me, that is, in my sinful nature. For I have the desire to do what is good, but I cannot carry it out. For what I do is not the good I want to do; no, the evil I do not want to do—this I keep on doing." (Romans 7:18-19)

Why do we feel that way? Is temptation sin?
   Desired Response: We tend to think that being tempted to do wrong is in itself wrong.

Let's look at a story in the Bible to find out...

CONTENT:

Does anyone remember the story of Joseph and how he dealt with Potiphar's wife?
   Desired Response: If yes, let someone give a brief retelling. If not, read the story from Scripture.

Genesis 39 (Today's English Version)

Now the Ishmaelites had taken Joseph to Egypt and sold him to Potiphar, one of the king's officers, who was the captain of the palace guard. The Lord was with Joseph and made him successful. He lived in the house of his Egyptian master, who saw that the Lord was with Joseph and had made him successful in everything he did. Potiphar was pleased with him and made him his personal servant; so he put him in charge of his house and everything he owned. From then on, because of Joseph the Lord blessed the household of the Egyptian and everything that he had in his house and in his fields. Potiphar turned over everything he had to the care of Joseph and did not concern himself with anything except the food he ate.

Joseph was well built and good-looking, and after a while his master's wife began to desire Joseph and asked him to go to bed with her. He refused and said to her, "Look, my master does not have to concern himself with anything in the house, because I am here. He has put me in charge of everything he has. I have as much authority in this house as he has, and he has not kept back anything from me except you. How then could I do such an immoral thing and sin against God?" Although she asked Joseph day after day, he would not go to bed with her.

But one day when Joseph went into the house to do his work, none of the house servants were there. She caught him by his robe and said, "Come to bed with me." But he escaped and ran outside, leaving his robe in her hand. When she saw that he had left his robe and had run out of the house, she called to her house servants and said, "Look at this! This Hebrew that my husband brought to the house is insulting us. He came into my room and tried to rape me but I screamed as loud as I could. When he heard me scream, he ran outside, leaving his robe beside me."

She kept his robe with her until Joseph's master cam home. Then she told him the same story: "That Hebrew slave that you brought here came into my room and insulted me. But when I screamed, he ran outside, leaving his robe beside me."

Joseph's master was furious and had Joseph arrested and put in the prison where the king's prisoners were kept, and there he stayed. But the Lord was with Joseph and blessed him, so that the jailer was pleased with him. He put Joseph in charge of all the other prisoners and made him responsible for everything that was done in the prison. The jailer did not have to look after anything for which Joseph was responsible, because the Lord was with Joseph and made him succeed in everything he did.

AFTER THE READING:

What did Joseph do wrong? Anything?

Desired Response: Joseph didn't do anything wrong.

What did he do right? How did Joseph deal with temptation?

Desired Response: He got out of there, ran away. ("Resist the devil and he will flee from you."-James 4:7)

How was he prepared in advance?

Desired Response: He had focused his life on God and stayed faithful. ("Set your mind on things above, not on earthly things."—Colossians 3:2-3)

Did he feel guilty about being tempted? What did he do as a last result?

Desired Response: No, he ran away! He even left his clothes behind! (God is faithful. He will not let you be tempted beyond what you can bear. But when you are tempted, he will also provide a way out so that you can stand up under it. —1 Corinthians 10:13)

There's a difference between temptation and sin. Joseph was tempted, did not feel guilty about it, and did not sin. He counted the cost. He figured out that giving into temptation was not worth the cost.

FINDING A FOCUS

THE POINT: When presented with temptation, if we engage with the temptation or even dwell on fighting it, we will probably fail. The path away from temptation involves refocusing on Jesus.

SUMMARY: Participants watch a sketch that demonstrates the importance of focusing on God rather than our temptations.

TIME NEEDED: 10 minutes

MATERIALS: Belt

Cross (in room somewhere for alternate focus point)

ROLES NEEDED: Teacher

Tempter (Uses the belt to "tempt" the teacher)

INTRODUCTION:

POINT: Temptation is not sin

We have a very real enemy, and he will try to make us feel guilty for being tempted. Even Jesus was tempted and those feelings are not wrong.

It's important to distinguish between temptation and sin. Sexual temptation, for example, isn't the same as acting on that sexual impulse. We often feel guilty when we're being tempted-as if there's something wrong with us, or that we need to confess temptation as if it were sin.

POINT: We have some tools to deal with temptation.

The first tool we have is to take action (as Joseph did). We need to take temptation seriously enough to do something about it. Do everything you can to get yourself out of the situation, ask God into the situation, listen to his counsel, call a friend. Any of these will work better than just trying to "will" it away.

The second tool is to FOCUS on JESUS. We must pursue Jesus as the one who rescues and comes to our aid. Here's what that may look like:

Stage: Draw an imaginary line in front of you.

Jesus is next to us. He's on our side—on "this side of the line." Jesus is our advocate and intercessor. But he doesn't cross over the line to being against us just because we're tempted—or even if we sin.

CONTENT:

Stage: Have a student dangle a bright belt in front of the teacher's eyes as he/she begins to talk about focus—and make sure it's between the teacher and the cross. Make it impossible to ignore and increasingly obnoxious. Make every attempt to get the teacher's attention.

Let's say I have a passion for belts. It's right in front of my eyes. If I allow all of my focus to be fixed on the belt, then my focus is only on fighting against my desire for the belt. Getting the focus off of the temptation and onto something else will help. What happens if all I do is look at the temptation?

Desired Response: It gets harder to resist.

What happens if I focus on the cross? Then I'm saying, "Wow, there's a belt dangling in front of me, and I'd really like to have it. Yup, it's really tempting. But I'm going to decide to stop looking at the belt and instead look over here!"

Stage: Point to the cross and keep your focus there.

If I pray and bring God into the situation and concentrate on him—what he says he provides and what he says about me—and if I stop concentrating on what I can't have, then I stand a chance of winning. I not only have been distracted away from the temptation, but I now have all the resources and power of God on my side.

WRAP-UP:

 POINT: Engaging with the temptation can lead to sin.

Have you ever tried concentrating on NOT eating chocolate cake? It's pretty hard! The more you think about it, the more you have to have it. The best way out is to focus on the cross, looking beyond the temptation. If you have to let it swing in front of your eyes, admit your weakness and then focus on the cross.

POINT: Every urge, feeling, or temptation doesn't have to be entertained.

Some thoughts and feelings need to go right on through our brains or hearts. We don't stop to fight them, acknowledge them, or even attribute them to ourselves or God or the enemy. If feelings tempt us, we don't have to own them—we can just let them go. We readily recognize that Satan will sometimes lie to us in thoughts that aren't really our own. Or feelings. Did you know that feelings can be from Satan as well? Not all feelings are true nor do they have to be followed.

POINT: Feeling guilty for being tempted is a trap that robs us of our focus on Jesus.

As we focus on the cross and Jesus, we must recognize that guilt under the addiction or temptation may rise up and distract us. We can deal with that at the cross, too. That may be what's driving the temptation (or addiction).

Focus is one of the strongest tools we have in the war against temptation: *"Set your mind on things above, not on earthly things."* (Colossians 3:2)

TESTIMONY:

Arrange for someone to offer a brief testimony about living with temptation.

Testimony Example: I was volunteering in ministry and was attracted to a ministry leader. Of course the attraction was completely one-sided, and I was quite careful to not reveal it and, most definitely, to not act on it in any way. In fact, I avoided being with this ministry leader (which was a wise move). But I did not totally run away—I had to keep working with this person.

So I decided to try a different approach. This time I realized that I wasn't going to be ashamed, and I wasn't going to feel guilty about the attraction, either. Nor was I going to pursue the person or the act on the attraction. I could learn to have the intense feelings I was having and NOT be ashamed but NOT give in, either. I began learning to constantly place those feelings at the foot of the cross and give them to Jesus. The temptation was not sin, although my response could be. I had to let the feelings happen in front of Jesus and focus on Jesus, not the temptation. THAT was incredibly hard. "Okay Jesus, I'm having these feelings RIGHT NOW. I'm not ashamed of the feelings, I'm not going to deny them or revel in them. But I admit them to you and stand in front of you until they subside. Lord, HELP!"

And that's what I did. I focused on Jesus—and on doing SOMETHING ELSE.

We also need to lean on our other relationships as we battle temptation. As we strive to live our lives for God and avoid giving in to our temptations, we often need to find trusted Christian friends who can help us to stay strong. Our challenge is to find others whom we can trust to share struggles with. Ask them to check in with you about how you are doing in this area (a.k.a. hold you accountable). Sometimes, just knowing someone will be asking if we drank at the party or went too far with our girlfriends or boyfriends keeps us from giving into temptation.

THE PAIN/PLEASURE BALANCE

THE POINT: We all live with a balance of pain and pleasure. When pain increases, we look to offset it with pleasure. Since pain continually hits us, we look to repeat the actions that brought us pleasure.

SUMMARY: Using a balance scale, the leader demonstrates how when painful things happen in our lives (adding weight to one side) we respond by trying to offset the pain with pleasure (adding weights to the other side).

TIME NEEDED: 5 minutes

MATERIALS: Balance scale or something made to imitate one
Weights (pennies are good) to drop onto the scale

INTRODUCTION:

If you give into temptation often enough, you'll have less and less control over your response to that temptation down the road. And this can lead to addiction. All temptations don't necessarily lead to addiction, but all addictions are born of temptations that weren't successfully resisted.
How does this work and why?

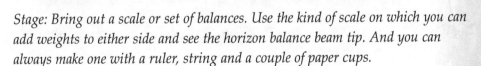

POINT: We look for pleasure to compensate for pain.

Stage: Bring out a scale or set of balances. Use the kind of scale on which you can add weights to either side and see the horizon balance beam tip. And you can always make one with a ruler, string and a couple of paper cups.

We always maintain a balance in our emotional and physical lives. This balance is between pain and pleasure. When we get hit by something painful, be it abuse or deprivation...

Stage: Toss some weights into scale to get it out of balance.

...We will naturally seek ways to regain balance or equilibrium.

Stage: Toss some weights into scale to get it back into balance.

The more pain we feel, the more pleasure we look for to compensate. When we're in pain, then our need to compensate rises up. How many of you want to eat when you get stressed? Eating is a pleasure that we often use to compensate for pain and difficulty in our lives.

WRAP-UP:

Pain prompts us to seek to pleasurable activities or objects. Having been hit broadside by some hurtful reality, we seek out pleasure in order to crowd out whatever unpleasant emotional state we find ourselves in. Pleasure rewards us by helping us to displace the pain.

> POINT: If we find something pleasurable, we'll look to repeat that pleasure when hit with pain.

When pain arises again, we tend to opt for the release that the object of pleasure affords us. Before long, our systems can't function well without the pleasurable release. We all respond to pain with an attempt to reduce it or to cover it over with something else to compensate for it. This is the root of compulsive behaviors —we try to deal with pain in inappropriate ways. And because we are creatures of habit, we look to try to reproduce the same results with repeated behavior.

Studies show that what drugs do is stimulate the pleasure sense. They stimulate this sense so much that other things that used to be pleasurable don't compare to the artificially stimulated pleasure that drugs produce.

THE CYCLE OF ADDICTION

THE POINT: Addiction is our attempt to deal with pain—except we become trapped by it.

SUMMARY: A leader uses overheads to walk the group through the cycle of addiction.

TIME NEEDED: 30 minutes

MATERIALS: The group needs to view the cycle of addiction as a group. This can be accomplished through a PowerPoint presentation, overhead transparency, whiteboard/chalk board, or newsprint.

Copies of **The Cycle of Addiction** repro page (page 123)

INTRODUCTION:

We are going to be talking about addictions. Addictions occur when we fall prey to temptations on a habitual basis in our attempt to deal with pain. When you think of addictions, what kinds of things come to mind?

Desired Response: Prompt only enough to have the group start to call out addictions.

COMMON ADDICTIONS CAN INVOLVE:

Approval	Attractiveness	Being good	Being helpful
Being right	Calendars	Cars	Chocolate
Cleanliness	Coffee	Computers	Drinking
Drugs	Overeating	Envy	Exercise
Fantasies	Friends	Gambling	Gardening
Gossiping	Guilt	Housekeeping	Humor
Ice cream	Knowledge	Messiness	Money
Movies	Music	Performance	Pizza
Potato chips	Power	Punctuality	Seductiveness
Sex	Shoplifting	Sports	Sunbathing
Television	Tobacco	Video Games	Weight lifting
Work			

Are these things wrong in and of themselves? Some yes, some no. But they all produce some sort of pleasurable response to us.

We can all think of examples, but how would you define what addiction is?
Desired Response: Have group attempt to define addictions. End when you get "close enough."

Here's the sophisticated definition: Any compulsive, habitual human behavior that limits the freedom of human desire. It is caused by the attachment of desire to specific objects.

The addiction really refers to the compulsiveness of the behavior and our inability to get out of it. Because we are unable to stop, our freedom is limited.

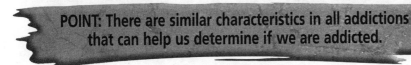

POINT: There are similar characteristics in all addictions that can help us determine if we are addicted.

OKAY, SO HOW DO YOU KNOW IF YOU HAVE AN ADDICTION?

1. TOLERANCE:

We always want more. We get used to the effects of a certain amount of the behavior and get accustomed to its presence in our lives. We move to a new level of equilibrium so when pain comes and we respond with our need for pleasure, we have to go to new extremes to obtain it since the old pleasure is now part of the norm.

2. WITHDRAWAL SYMPTOMS:

NOT doing what we're addicted to causes some stress. We may have backlash reactions. If I'm addicted to having others always feel good about me, and I know that someone has a problem with me, I may overreact and feel especially bad. What's happening is that the lack of repeated pleasure upsets the pain/pleasure balance, putting me back to compensating for the pain.

3. SELF-DECEPTION:

Our mind plays tricks to get us to continue the addiction. We deny that we have a problem, or we make up excuses and rationalize. A guy might say, "A little porn doesn't hurt so long as I'm the only one affected." The real issue is that we need the pleasurable release.

4. LOSS OF WILLPOWER:

We find ourselves powerless to stop. Why? Because we have mixed motives, a part of us really wants the pleasurable release.

What's the best test to find out if you are struggling with an addiction? Go ahead and just stop it. If you are successful, there is no addiction. If you aren't successful, no amount of rationalization will change the fact of the addiction being there.

POINT: Addictions develop into a full cycle that reinforces the pattern.

Okay, so how does an addiction develop?

Stage: Pass out **The Cycle of Addiction** *repro page. Get a volunteer to play Mary in the skit. Give "Mary" a copy of the following description of the addiction cycle and examples from Mary's life. Following the description of each step in the cycle, let the volunteer act out the example about Mary's evening at home. At the end of the step, the volunteer should freeze (as if a video tape was paused) until the next step. (Feel free to replace the example of Mary with another example of another person dealing with a different addictive cycle, as is appropriate to your group).*

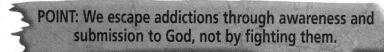

POINT: We escape addictions through awareness and submission to God, not by fighting them.

Okay, so now what? The way out is the way through....

"Do not be overcome by evil, but overcome evil with good." (Romans 12:21)

HERE'S WHAT WE NEED TO DO:

1. BECOME AWARE OF THE ADDICTION
- Admit your powerlessness to overcome the addiction by yourself (the first step of any 12-step program).
- Recognize God's grace in the midst of failure.
- Stop rationalizing the situation (denials, running away, ignoring it).

2. COME BEFORE GOD IN HONESTY
- Admit to God the behavior and its sinfulness.
- Remember that God loves you despite the behavior and forgives sin, no matter how frequently it is committed.

3. ALLOW GOD'S PRESENCE TO MINISTER TO THE PAIN

- When we stop an addiction, the withdrawal symptoms kick in, and both the pain of lack of the pleasure and the underlying pain will come up. Be willing to go to the cross with your pain. There may be new unhealed areas that come to the surface that have been covered over. Get prayer from others and be willing to deal with the pain.

4. BECOME AWARE OF THE TRIGGERS

- Know when you're becoming vulnerable to your addiction and get others to pray for you.

5. DEVELOP HEALTHY ALTERNATIVES

- At the point when we walk down well-worn paths toward sin, we need other actions to take. Call someone, take a walk, engage in other activities, schedule your life knowing your difficult times. Plan it in advance.

6. AFTER A FAILURE

- Understand the forgiveness and cleansing of God.
- Take failure as a way to work humility and dependence.
- Get prayer from others.

7. RECOGNIZE THAT GOD HAS BUILT-IN OUR INCOMPLETENESS.

- Realize that we'll hunger for God all of our days and be incomplete until we get to heaven.
- Be hungry for more of God. Holy hunger for God can result in a purer desire for him than ever!

WRAP-UP:

A final word. We're going to have to deal with pain until we arrive in heaven. Pain shouldn't drive us from God or make us give up. Pain should instead drive us to God!

"For the creation was subjected to frustration, not by its own choice, but by the will of the one who subjected it, in hope that the creation itself will be liberated from its bondage to decay and brought into the glorious freedom of children of God." (Romans 8:20-21)

"For while we are in this tent [or body], we groan and are burdened, because we do not wish to be unclothed but to be clothed with our heavenly dwelling, so that what is mortal may be swallowed up by life. Now it is God who has made us for this very purpose and has given us the Spirit as a deposit, guaranteeing what is to come."
(2 Corinthians 5:4-5)

Addiction can lead you to frustration, guilt, despair, and ultimately away from God. On the other hand, addiction can lead you to absolute dependence on God, to getting beyond the place of shame to living in forgiveness and grace.

THE CHOICE IS YOURS!

POSSIBLE SMALL GROUP QUESTIONS

SMALL GROUP GOALS:

- Pray for forgiveness in areas of failure.
- Pray for strengthening for areas of weakness.
- Pray for passion for Jesus so that we can focus.

1. How do you deal with temptation? Do you fight hard or do you give in?
2. What else could you do to avoid giving into temptation?
3. When we talk about having your feelings of temptation in front of Jesus, how does that strike you? No big deal, or a great big challenge? How hard/easy is it for you to be really real in front of Jesus?
4. What areas of temptation do you need prayer about?
5. Do you see yourself having repeating patterns of sin in your life? Can you call this addiction or not?
6. What are the triggers for you?
7. Does it seem like you have a choice in acting on the trigger?
8. What wedges could you put between triggers/temptations and acting on them?
9. What creative alternatives can you use when hit by a trigger?

INDIVIDUAL CHALLENGE AS A RESULT:

- I will refuse to feel guilt and shame when I'm tempted and pursue Jesus instead.
- I will take whatever steps necessary to have options that squelch temptation and stop the cycle of addiction.
- I will pursue accountability.

RESOURCES AND REFERENCES

RELATED SCRIPTURES:

Genesis 39
Matthew 4:1-11
1 Corinthians 10:13
Colossians 3:1-3
James 4:7
1 Peter 5:8
Romans 7:18-19

OUTSIDE REFERENCE MATERIALS:

Gerald May, *Addiction and Grace* (San Francisco: Harper, 1991). Drawing on his experience as a psychiatrist working with chemically dependent individuals, May details the various addictions from which we suffer. He examines the "processes of attachment" that leads to addiction and describes the relationship between addiction and spiritual awareness. Heavy going but excellent material.

Don Williams, *Jesus and Addiction* (Recovery Publications, 1993).
A good but more basic treatment of addiction.

THE CYCLE OF ADDICTION

1. TRIGGER: Something in us kicks in so we begin thinking about the object of our desire. This could be a painful situation that creates the need for pleasure to stay in balance or could be the normal stuff of temptation that comes our way. Remember that many triggers are simply temptations and should not be things we feel guilty over.

> *Example: Mary is sitting home on a Friday night, alone, watching a movie. The fairy tale romance in the movie reminds her of how much she wants to have the perfect relationship with the perfect guy, and Mary starts to feel lonely and depressed...*

2. CHOICE: We have a choice after being triggered. We can choose a different path, or we can choose to fall into the cycle. Once addictions get established, we face a loss of willpower in being able to choose to do something other than fall.

> *Example: Mary knows that this feeling often sends her into depression. She knows she could call someone from the youth group to talk with her and pray for her, but "it's late" and she "might wake someone up."*

3. PREOCCUPATION: We become preoccupied with the object of our addiction. We can think of nothing but how good it will feel to give in to our desire. If we don't make a choice to not give in, we will begin to make plans in order to get to the point of release.

> *Example: Mary thinks, "I bet I'd feel better if I had something to eat. Ice cream, and lots of it, always makes me feel better."*

4. PLANNING: We start to anticipate the behavior and recall how good it will feel. A certain euphoria sets in. This can involve very habitual patterns of thought life or fantasy. Some people have very specific routines in order to build up excitement prior to the actual release.

> *Example: Mary remembers that there's a full container of cookie dough ice cream in the freezer and some chocolate cake. She imagines getting a great big bowl of it and a slice of cake to go with it. She sighs, imagining the pleasure she will feel while eating the food....*

5. RELEASE: We do the behavior itself and experience the rush of pleasure associated. That pleasure however is fleeting.

> *Example: Mary goes downstairs and prepares her "late night snack." She takes it back to her room and eats the whole thing.*

6. SHAME AND GUILT: Once we realize we have fallen again, we heap shame on ourselves and feel detached from God and from others. The shame and guilt convince us that we're "bad" and actually produce more pain that triggers the need for pleasure to balance it all over again!

> *Example: Mary puts the dish down, feeling a bit sick to her stomach. What she did starts to set in. "I am such a pig! No wonder 'Mr. Right' hasn't come along! He wouldn't want someone like me! I am so stupid and so totally out of control."*

7. THE ROOT NEED IS IGNORED: Often we're absorbed in the addiction itself or in fighting the addiction, so we don't ever look beyond the behavior to the underlying issues.

WHERE DO I END & WHERE DO YOU BEGIN?

HOW BOUNDARIES AFFECT...EVERYTHING!

MAIN POINTS:

1. A boundary tells me where I end and you begin.

2. Setting boundaries involves:
   My "stuff," my emotions, and my personal history
   My choices
   My responsibilities

3. When we start setting boundaries, we need to check our motivations and attitudes.

4. God's healing in the area of personal boundaries is a process.

5. God wants to restore broken boundaries and strengthen us in weak places.

LESSON SEGMENTS:

What's Mine & What's Yours
"Me & Others" Role-plays
Where Are You?

IN THIS LESSON...

Learning how to set boundaries in your life...

Discovering how "bad boundaries" affect your relationships...

Encountering God's healing where your boundaries have been broken...

WHAT'S MINE AND WHAT'S YOURS

THE POINT: Defining a "boundary"—defining what's mine and what's yours is a major task on the road to healthy relationships.

SUMMARY: A large floor diagram illustrates what is "mine" and what "belongs to others." As we progress through the lesson, we add things to the illustration on the floor so participants can see what they should "own"—their own attitudes, emotions, actions, thoughts, choices, and responsibilities.

TIME NEEDED: 20 Minutes

MATERIALS: Masking tape
30 sheets of paper
3 sheets of $8^1/_2$ x 14 paper to name the boundary areas (write "Physical/Sexual" on one, "Emotional" on another, and "Intellectual" on the last.)
6 large sheets of paper (poster size)
  • Two papers with † on them over an arrow
  • One paper with a cross on it
  • One paper with "ME" on it
  • One paper with "Other" on it
3 markers (one for leader, 2 for scribes)
Baby gate set between two chairs or something to act as a door to the room

ROLES NEEDED: Several student scribes
Student to act as camper

PREPARATION: Outline the borders of the room with masking tape. Make the room at least 10 feet per side. Use a space where no one's sitting. Appoint several scribes and ask them to write as you direct them.

INTRODUCTION:

We're going to talk about boundaries. We'll define that in a few minutes. First, let's jump into an illustration. I need a volunteer to be a camper.

Stage: Invite someone to play the role of a camper.

What if I tell you all that we're going on a hike? Each of you is responsible to carry your own water and food for the trip. It'll be a long hike, but I know you can make it.

Say our camper here is all packed with food and water and ready for the hike, and I come up and ask if our camper can carry my water. And then others ask our camper to carry their food. And one after the other, all sorts of people give our camper their stuff to carry.

How do you think our camper is feeling? How well can our camper take care of things if everyone else is burdening our camper?

Desired Response: The camper feels overwhelmed and used. The camper can't carry everyone else's stuff, plus his/her own stuff. The camper will probably get exhausted on the trip because of all the extra burdens.

Our lives are a journey—kind of like a hike—during which we're responsible to take care of our own stuff. We must own and take care of our own thoughts, feelings, actions, and bodies. Just like our camper would have gotten in trouble on the hike by carrying everyone else's food and water, we get in trouble in our lives when we make ourselves responsible for others' feelings and actions. We get exhausted from feeling responsible for others' emotions and end up neglecting our own.

Now, we want to help our friends, and we care about their feelings and what they do. Can someone give an example of the difference between helping a friend out (being a good friend) and being responsible for their feelings and actions in an unhealthy way?

Desired Response: Allow for time for them to respond with some examples.

It seems so biblical to ditch your own needs in favor of another's. But when we make it our responsibility to fix, control, or protect another person, we can cut God out of the picture. We need to be connected to God and led by his Spirit. When we try to be responsible for how someone else feels or acts, we become connected to the other person and controlled by a sense of duty or guilt. God does lead us to care for one another in sacrificial ways—but it must be God's leading, not guilt or our own need to fix them or take care of them.

How can we make sure that we're not taking on so much of others' stuff that we get wiped out and forget about our own needs? It's all about setting boundaries.

CONTENT:

What is a boundary?

> **POINT: A boundary separates you from me. It tells me where I end and you begin.**

Henry Cloud and John Townsend say that a boundary is like a property line. We initially learn boundaries in the terrible twos—beginning about 18 months of age-and learning them is absolutely vital! If we're not given freedom then or invited to begin to explore the limits, we lose something incredibly crucial.

Stage: Show property line and add paper on floor with "me" and "others."

What does a boundary do?
a) Keeps me from hurting others
b) Keeps others from hurting me

ME	OTHERS

While doing for others is a Christian principle, you'll be hard pressed to find biblical examples of Jesus doing a good deed against someone's will. When Jesus told the rich young ruler to sell everything and give it to the poor, he went away disappointed. (Mark 10:20-22) Nowhere does it indicate that Jesus pursued him to try to convince him, argue the point, or get him to come back. God is absolutely committed to our free will and will not crush our decisions. He's far more committed to respect individual choices—even the bad ones—than we are with the kids in our groups! We need to know when to allow teenagers to make their own decisions and let them go, rather than pursuing them at all costs, based on our need to see them change.

Stage: Illustrate on floor with the papers with † and arrows over the boundary.

Does this room have solid walls?
  Desired Response: No.

That's right. This is a doorway—and we often pretend it isn't there.

  Stage: Set up gate between two chairs. Make sure it can be moved.
  Start with it open.

Who put it there?
  Desired Response: God—but sometimes we could also say we learn to have it,
  or our parents show us, or we put it there.

POINT: We aren't born with good boundaries—we learn them. Boundaries show us who to let through the door. And if we don't learn that from Mom and Dad, we'll have a harder time closing our door later.

The door goes both ways—and it's okay to know who to allow in and who to keep out. This door allows us to control our boundaries. Unfortunately, it's not a very good door for some of us. If these boundaries have been broken by abuse, we often continue to let people pour stuff over the boundary line into our hearts—bad stuff coming in, just like the abuse was a violation. For other people it's locked so tight that no one can visit. We erect a very sturdy door to keep all the people who could help OUT.

When is it okay to let others through the door?
  Desired Response: When that person is Jesus. When we decide a person is safe.
  It's up to us if we want to say yes. It is OUR door. No one has a right to abuse
  that. If they have abused it, it is WRONG—regardless of whether we said they
  could come in or not!

What kinds of boundaries are there?

There are lots of boundaries out there, but there are three in particular that we want to talk about: Sexual, emotional, and intellectual.

  Stage: Place 8 ½ x14 sheets of paper labeled "Sexual," "Emotional," and
  "Intellectual" along the boundary line as you discuss each. Discuss as briefly as
  possible; the information below is background if you need it. Basically just cover
  what each boundary is and what it does.

SEXUAL:
What does breaking this boundary look like?
  Any physical abuse, any sexual abuse, making someone sexually
  uncomfortable, and neglect.

Results of this boundary being broken:
- Shame (but sometimes with loyalty to the abuser).
- Feeling that setting boundaries is betrayal.

Or in the case of neglect:
- The need for physical affection, and no established boundary at all.

EMOTIONAL:

What are your feelings, and what are mine? Emotional boundaries allow us to protect our emotional selves. They let us know what emotions we can deflect and what emotions we own as ours.

What does breaking someone's emotional boundaries look like?
- When one person passes all emotions to another and expects that person to feel the same way.
- When parents or other authority figures look to children to meet their own needs—or when adults tell children inappropriate information. (For example, it's never okay for a mother to confide in a child the problems she may be having in her marriage.)
- Role reversal. A very common one is when parents look to their children to take care of them—where the child must help the parent's feelings or must not do anything that upsets the parent.
- Shaming and humiliation including taunting and name-calling.

Results of broken boundaries:
- We cannot become our own person. We end up expressing other people's emotions for them.
- We cannot feel our own feelings, only what the other person allows. This can lead to emotional shutdown and believing our feelings are dangerous or wrong.
- We're like an emotional sponge with no separateness. We soak up feelings around us and allow others to determine our emotions and then get confused about why we feel the way we do.
- With shaming, we end up with a "critical committee" in our heads all the time so that we can never feel good about ourselves.

INTELLECTUAL:

What do I believe versus what do you believe? We learn to trust how to view the world.

What does breaking this boundary look like?
- Blurred boundaries with people who too tightly control what to think.

Results of this boundary being broken:
- We want others to think for us. (e.g., "Don't cross the street, it scares me to death," versus "Don't cross the street, it's dangerous." Or, "You know you'll feel better if you wear that shirt"—so I wear it not because I like it, but because you do.)

What are boundaries made of?

Lots of things, but at least these:
- Skin
- Time (e.g., time off from a relationship, etc.)
- Geographical space and distance
- Words
- Truth (God's truth and the truth about yourself)
- Support from others

All of these can be the building material for a boundary.

What does setting boundaries involve?

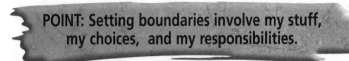

POINT: Setting boundaries involve my stuff, my choices, and my responsibilities.

Stage: Ask scribes to write these down and place them in appropriate places on the floor—see your diagram.

1. Keeping my stuff in my space and your stuff out.

Stage: Ask scribes to label one side of floor "my stuff," and the other side "not my stuff."

What's my stuff? The things in my space.

Stage: Ask scribes to write each of the below actions and attitudes on pieces of paper and drop each piece of paper on the appropriate side as you discuss it or mention it.

Attitudes
Actions
Emotions
Behaviors and consequences
Choices
Values
Limits
Talents
Thoughts
Desires
Love

What's other people's stuff? All the same things—but theirs, not mine (e.g., their emotions, their choices, etc.)

Stage: Scribes write "their actions, emotions, attitudes," et cetera and put them in the "not my stuff" section.

The next two we are going to say are door-keeping functions:

Stage: Ask scribes to write these down and place them in appropriate place on the floor—see diagram. Add sheets of paper that say, "their choices, their responsibilities" as well.

2. Making choices and allowing others to make choices instead of being controlled, or fearful, or manipulating or taking control.

    That means that in any given situation, there are choices to be made—and consequences to those choices. I am responsible to make my choices. For example: *Will I go to school and take the test in Algebra and then get to go to the mall tonight? Or will I skip school, blow off my test, go to the mall instead, and lose my car privileges for a month?* Those are choices with appropriate consequences. Mom probably said, "Susie, if you go to school and get through the test, you can still go to the mall tonight—but if you don't go to school, I'm taking away your car privileges for a month," and you weighed the alternatives. "Let's see... a month? Not worth it. A week? Probably worth it. A day? I'm going to the mall NOW!" *Manipulation* would be if Mom said, "Susie, it will really look bad to Jennifer's mom if you don't get an A on that test." *Control* might be if I said, "Tiffany, you have to take me to the mall today—you're the only one I can count on to tell my mom I was at school!" A fear reaction might look like this: "I know that I'm supposed to be in school today, but I'm too afraid to take this final. I just know I'm not going to get a good grade, and Mom will annihilate me! It's worth losing privileges to not have to face that test."

We cannot make anyone do anything. We can only make choices for ourselves.
- I can't make anyone do anything.
- Parents can't make anyone do anything.
- God won't make anyone do anything.

We make choices and there are consequences for our behavior.

3. Being responsible *to*...not responsible *for* people. This is a hard one to understand! Basically, we all have responsibilities to one another. We are responsible to communicate and engage in relationships, to love one another (which is to value one another, not necessarily to trust one another or do everything for one another), and to care for and help one another...but within limits! We are not to be responsible for others. We allow others to take responsibility for themselves and for their own decisions.

WRAP-UP:

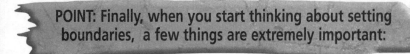

POINT: Finally, when you start thinking about setting boundaries, a few things are extremely important:

MOTIVATION:

Many times our choices are based on fear, and God never wants us to act out of fear. Appropriate anxiety is different from fear that our needs won't be met. ("God has not given us a spirit of fear."—2 Timothy 1:7)

This is the difference between...

a) Not jumping off the curb without looking-which is "appropriate anxiety"
and
b) Not crossing the street ever because we're afraid of being hit by a car—which is fear.

ATTITUDE:

Boundaries applied in frustration or anger will be interpreted wrongly. It's better to deal with the anger first and then set the boundary so the other person doesn't wonder what avalanche just hit them.

Now that we've seen whose is what, it's time for some examples.

"ME AND OTHERS" ROLE-PLAYS

THE POINT: We have to practice setting boundaries to find out what's mine and what's someone else's.

SUMMARY: Role-plays are used to show unhealthy relationships with bad boundaries. We discuss who is boundary-less and suggest ways to correct the situation.

TIME NEEDED: 25 minutes

MATERIALS: Role-play descriptions for players (page 138)

ROLES NEEDED: See forthcoming descriptions.
Maximum 8 players, at least 2 pairs should be opposite sex

INTRODUCTION:

We're going to look at some scenarios now—in fact, YOU are going to act them out! I have 4 sketches here. Each needs two actors.

Stage: Ask students to pick two of the four sketches at random—without seeing their subject. Or pick two that are most appropriate. Give repro pages to the groups as you choose them. Give them 5 to 6 minutes to quickly decide how to play the scene (but tell them 3 minutes!). Remind them these are SHORT sketches—no more than 1 1/2 minutes MAX! Then ask them to act out scenes. Lead a discussion about the sketches after they act them out.

You have 3 minutes to figure out the scene and try it. Go!

CONTENT:

ROLE-PLAY #1 (Woman and child) debrief questions:

➤ What's going on?
> *Desired Response: Mom's given up something here. And she's taken on a responsibility that's not hers.*

➤ Who's controlling whom here?
> *Desired Response: Mom probably thinks she's controlling things, but the kid is actually controlling mom.*

➤ Who's responsible for the room?
> *Desired Response: Child.*

➤ Who is mom making responsible for the room?
> *Desired Response: Herself.*

➤ She is trying to do what to the child?
> *Desired Response: Trying to regain control.*

➤ Who should have the responsibility here?
> *Desired Response: Child.*

➤ Who has a boundary problem here?
> *Desired Response: Probably both—child is manipulating mom.*

➤ What attitudes and actions are ending up on the wrong side of this boundary? Where is the choice? Where is the responsibility?

➤ What would be a better way of working this out so the child has choices, and the mom doesn't have to manipulate or threaten?
> *Desired Response: Many options. Elicit some.*
> *Here's one suggestion, below...*

POSSIBLE SOLUTION:
> Mom: "You're right, honey. I've said that lots of times, and I shouldn't have said it unless I meant it. Tell you what. I'll finish helping today, but let's make a deal. From now on, you clean the room. It's already supposed to be part of how you earn your allowance. And if you don't, then we'll take $1.00 off your allowance every week that you don't clean it."

ROLE-PLAY #2 (high school/college guy and girl) **debrief questions:**

➤ What's going on? Who's controlling whom here?
> *Desired Response: Guy manipulating girl to get what he wants.*

➤ What about choices? Is there respect for choices here?
> *Desired Response: No. This is manipulation. He's taking away her right to choose.*

➤ What is the guy giving up?
> *Desired Response: His responsibility to make his own decision wisely and put limits on himself.*

➤ What is the girl giving up?
> *Desired Response: Her responsibility and her resolution—and therefore, her decision. His manipulation is abusive and a power play.*

➤ Who is boundary-less here?
> *Desired Response: Both.*

➤ How could this be replayed to give them proper responsibility and choices?

Stage: Solicit responses. Could be lots of options—like the one below.

POSSIBLE SOLUTION:

Girl: "Look, I think that sex is really intimate and a really special thing. So I kind of want to save it for marriage, y'know? It's not that I don't love you; it's that I think we should save that for when we've made a lifelong commitment to each other."

Guy: "Sometimes this drives me crazy. I don't understand you. But I know how strongly you feel about this, and even though it will drive me nuts, I'm willing to wait for you. So I won't push you. But can we talk about it more later?"

ROLE-PLAY #3 (students) **debrief questions:**

➤ What's going on? Who's controlling whom?
> *Desired Response: Begging one is in control.*

➤ What is the victim giving up here?
> *Desired Response: Right to say no, to choose.*

➤ How is the begging student breaking a boundary?
> *Desired Response: Making the other one responsible for a burden that isn't theirs.*

Whose responsibility is the _____ (project, or whatever they're doing)?
Desired Response: The first kid.

Who are they trying to make responsible?
Desired Response: The other kid.

Who is boundary-less here?
Desired Response: Both.

How could this be replayed to give the two of them proper responsibility and choices?

Stage: Solicit responses. Could be lots of options-like the one below.

POSSIBLE SOLUTION:

First kid: "Look, I really need help. Do you know any way out of this situation?"

Other kid: "I'd love to help you, and I know this is a really important project for you, but I really can't take time off from _____right now. Have you considered talking to the (authority in the situation) to see if there are any good ideas available?"

ROLE-PLAY #4 (friends) debrief questions

What's going on here? Who's in control?
Desired Response: Friend #2.

What is friend #1 giving up?
Desired Response: That depends on how the scene is played. Probably nothing unless they're dangerous or manipulative and therefore unsafe for friend #2—in which case the "no" would be justified!

Who is boundary-less here?
Desired Response: Friend #2, who has walls, not boundaries, and is not letting the good of relationship inside.

Who's responsible for friend #2's problem?
Desired Response: Friend #2.

If Friend #1 started to really push, then would Friend #1 be boundary-less too?
Desired Response: YES! That person can't force the wall to come down.

How could this be replayed to give the two of them proper responsibility and choices?

Stage: Solicit responses. There could be lots of options—like the one below.

POSSIBLE SOLUTION:

> Friend #1: "You know, I really want to help and I care about you. So if it would help to talk, and you decide you'd like to, I'd be happy to listen."

> Friend #2. "Thanks. It's really hard to talk about this right now. I think I need some space. But could we talk in a couple of days? I'm really glad to know you're there. I'll give you a call, okay?"

WRAP-UP:

We are given opportunities every day to strengthen our boundaries and learn more about them! And we always have a choice (except in the case of ABUSE). So we have to decide whether the consequences (possible conflict and discomfort) are worth setting boundaries! Ultimately, setting appropriate boundaries is a healthier choice.

BOUNDARIES

THE POINT: God wants to overcome the weaknesses in our boundary setting and strengthen the weak places in our boundaries.

SUMMARY: We look at the chart on the floor and reflect on where we are, and what God wants to do to strengthen our boundaries.

TIME NEEDED: 10 minutes

MATERIALS: Create simple copies of blank "Me/Others" diagram, as shown on page 126.

INTRODUCTION:

Stage: Pass out repro pages of filled-in boundaries and blank outline of boundary.

There are lots of places where our boundaries can get broken or our door is swinging wide or our hearts have been trampled. God wants to heal those and enable you to work with him on rebuilding the walls (check out the biblical book of Nehemiah sometime—God knows all about rebuilding walls in our lives...he rebuilt a temple, after all!) Where is your heart with boundaries? What places does God want to strengthen? What does God want replace so he can put himself in as the new boundary, holding out his arms and showing you what the new boundary looks like?

CONTENT:

Take a few minutes and look at the floor and review what God showed you tonight. Are there boundaries he wants to set up in your life? Walls to take down? Limits you can set?

On the handout with the boundary outlined, draw where the boundaries in your life have been broken. Where is your heart? Inside the boundary? Where are the holes? Are there strong restored places? (There may be more than you think! God's probably been rebuilding the boundaries for a long time when you didn't know it!)

Where have you given up responsibility and control to others? Where can you start to make choices instead of being a victim or being controlling?

Stage: Leave as much time as needed for the writing of responses.

> **POINT: God is always at work, restoring the broken boundaries of our lives and offering us choices. He wants to set us free from the victimization and control, from the fear and the manipulation.**

God wants to show us how to strengthen our boundaries! Remember that we need to start this process slowly, or we'll scare everyone around us half to death! But where is God starting?

Let's pray...

PRAYER AND MINISTRY:

Father, we need latches on our doors. We have some strong places in our boundaries, but there are other places where the boundaries are weak. And there are places where there are big holes, and places where the door doesn't work, and places where we have wandered out of the place that you call OURS.

Lord, we confess we've let others walk all over our boundaries in various ways. Father, forgive us for not believing you aren't mad at us for the breaks in our walls, but you want to help rebuild them!

Lord, come and begin to restore—or put in place—the door that isn't working. In Jesus' name, we kick out all the cruddy things that have crept into our hearts and crossed our boundaries. We don't want them anymore, and we don't want to live with them. We renounce self-hatred, shame, condemnation, judgment, and all the things that go along with them.

We renounce fear, manipulation and control, and we confess the places where we have made other people responsible for "our stuff." Father, come and wash those places and make us firm and strong to not go there again.

And we choose to focus on you, Jesus. Come and stand as the gate, and protect the boundaries of our heart.

Amen.

POSSIBLE SMALL GROUP QUESTIONS

SMALL GROUP GOALS:

- Pray for the places where boundaries have been broken and need to be restored.

1. How is your door?
2. How do you feel when you have to say "no" to someone?
3. Where are your boundaries strong?
4. What do you do when you establish a boundary and someone doesn't respect it?
5. Do you give up quickly or do you stand up for your boundary?
6. Where are your boundaries weak?
7. What boundary areas would you like prayer for?

INDIVIDUAL COMMITMENT AS A RESULT:

- I will let God start to mend my boundaries and take down my self-made walls.
- I will make choices instead of controlling or being a victim, and take responsibility for what is mine.

RESOURCES AND REFERENCES

RELATED SCRIPTURE:

Ephesians 4:25
2 Corinthians 3:17-18
2 Corinthians 4:2
1 Peter 2:1
2 Timothy 1:7
The Book of Nehemiah—it relates the story of rebuilding the walls of Jerusalem with lots of good analogies throughout.

OUTSIDE REFERENCE MATERIALS:

Henry Cloud and John Townsend, *Boundaries* (Zondervan, 1992).
Also by Cloud and Townsend, *Boundaries with Kids*, *Boundaries in Dating*, and *Boundaries in Marriage*. Highly recommended series of books discussing boundaries. A must read!

Rokelle Lerner, *Boundaries for Codependents* (Hazelden Foundation, 1988).

Paul Meier, *Don't Let the Jerks Get the Best of You* (Thomas Nelson, 1995).

"ME AND OTHERS" ROLE-PLAYS

ROLE-PLAY #1:   CHARACTERS: MOM AND CHILD

Mom is cleaning room with or for child. She is complaining about the mess and how little the child is doing to help. Improvise dialogue—Mom is frustrated. Child is passive, not doing much. Include these lines in dialogue or end with something like this:

Mom: "This is the last time I'm cleaning up this room for you!"

Kid: "Oh Mom, you say that every week!"

ROLE-PLAY #2:   CHARACTERS: ONE MALE, ONE FEMALE

Guy and girl have been dating for a long time. Have talked about marriage but aren't ready for that commitment. Guy is pressuring girl about sex. Conversation ends in this kind of way:

Guy: "If you really loved me, you'd have sex with me."

Girl: "Well, I was going to wait until we got married, but I know you love me, and I love you, too, so..."

ROLE-PLAY #3:   CHARACTERS: 2 STUDENTS

One is begging the other to do something for a retreat weekend, or for a class project, or for a team, or for a club. The one with the need explains how much of a bind they're in and how much they need the other to help. The conversation gets more and more desperate—the first student is really counting on the other to say yes. (Don't manipulate or use guilt, it's more a begging and desperation situation.) The other wants to say no, but can't and gives in. Dialogue should include lines like:

One: "I'm so overwhelmed, I really, really need you to — *[some tedious chore or task related to the retreat, project, whatever]* for me."

The other: "I know, I know. That's okay, I was going to — *[something else that this speaker would rather do]*, but I'll just put it off again. I guess I can do it for you."

ROLE-PLAY #4:   CHARACTERS: 2 FRIENDS

Friend #1 sees that something is wrong with Friend #2. Friend #1 starts to ask if something is wrong, but Friend #2 won't respond. Friend #1 tries again, looking for other openings, gets mildly frustrated, but doesn't get mad at the Friend #2. Again Friend #1 tries gently to help, but Friend #2 won't allow it. Friend #2 is really denying there's anything wrong. Really avoiding the issue. Dialogue ends in this kind of way:

Friend #2: "It's really nothing, I'm fine. Besides, it's such a little thing...I think I just need to not think about it."

NOT JUST PLUMBING

REAL MASCULINITY AND FEMININITY IN A FALLEN WORLD

MAIN POINTS:

1. Men and women have similarities and differences. As male and female, we complement each other.

2. The images we see from culture, family, and peers help shape who we are as men and women. But these images can be a far cry from how God sees us.

3. Examples from Scripture give us clues about masculinity and femininity.

4. We all have both feminine and masculine characteristics. Women have a greater capacity for the feminine, and men for the masculine.

5. God wants to bless the characteristics we do have, and strengthen the ones that we have a greater capacity for and haven't developed.

IN THIS LESSON...

Understand the differences between masculine and feminine...

Receive God's blessing for who you are in your gender...

LESSON SEGMENTS:

Mary and David
Gender Continuum

MARY AND DAVID

THE POINT: Scriptural characters offer a glimpse into the qualities of masculine and feminine.

SUMMARY: Participants explore the masculine and feminine characteristics of Mary and David, Abraham, and others.

TIME NEEDED: 20 minutes

MATERIALS: Bibles, or Bible passages printed out
Overheads and markers to write down responses
Scripture references for the appropriate passages, written on small cards or paper to pass out

PREPARATION: In advance, pass out Scripture references that you wish to have read or paraphrased
(Choose from list below or use your own—reader may paraphrase)
Luke 1:38, 46-55 (Mary receptive to Lord's word, worships God)
Luke 2:19 (Mary ponders what she's seen and heard)
Proverbs 31:10-31 (Godly woman who is strong and wise and a business woman)
1 Sam 16:18 (said about David—warrior and musician)
1 Sam 13:14 (David is man after God's heart)
Hebrews 11:8-11, 17-19 (about Abraham as man of faith)

INTRODUCTION:

Tonight we're talking about gender. What is gender?
> *Desired response: Sex, male or female*

We're also talking about masculine and feminine. What's the difference—or is there any—between masculine and male?
> *Desired response: Male is the description of the person, masculine is a characteristic*

How many of you have heard the phrase from a book title, *Men Are from Mars, Women Are from Venus*?

What do you think of that title? Is it true? False? How?

Common theory today is that the differences between men and women are just plumbing…

> *Stage direction: Use one of the following examples about how many people believe there's really no underlying difference between men and women—or better yet your own testimony to the same effect.*

A) *There is a song in which a mom tries to raise her kids unisex: Boys play with dolls and girls mow the lawn. In the end she discovers her little boy playing with trucks in the dirt and her little girl wanting to bake him cookies. The song concludes: "Are they really like that, or are they just trying to stick it to Mom?"*

B) *From Life magazine, July 1999, pages 45-46, "What's the Difference Between Boys and Girls" by Deborah Blum.*

> *"My four-year-old son asked for a Barbie this year. His blue eyes were hopeful, his small face angelic. His mother was suspicious. My older son at one point began to see weapons in household objects the way adults dream up phallic symbols. 'Shoot her with the toothbrush,' he once shouted to a companion as they chased the cat around, the house. 'Why do you want the Barbie, honey?' I asked [my four year old]. 'I wanna chop her head off.'*

> *"There I was again, standing at the edge of the great gender divide, the place and the moment where one becomes absolutely sure that the opposite sex is, in fact, opposite. I know of no way for women of my generation, raised to believe in gender neutrality, to reach this edge faster than through trying to raise children.*

> *"'I did not do this,' a friend insisted on the day her son started carefully biting his toast into the shape of a gun. 'I think my daughter has a pink gene,' a British journalist confided recently, as she confessed that her daughter has not only a Barbie collection but all the matched plastic purses and tiny high-heeled shoes."*

Men and women are different—and that is GOOD.

Adam and Eve in the garden.
Were they the same? Different?
Was that okay before the fall? How about after the fall?

We are different, and that is okay.

> **POINT: Men and women have similarities and differences. As male and female, we complement each other.**

As far as men and women go, neither is better than the other—but together they offer something to the other that they can't receive on their own. They are the same, but they are different. They can do different things. They work together, but they aren't the same. They COMPLEMENT each other. They are counterparts to one another, with differences between them.

Random House definition:
> *Complementary:* Either of two parts or things needed to complete the whole; counterpart. Also: Something that completes or makes perfect: A good wine is a complement to a good meal.

In the end, who we look toward as models for what it means to be men and women matters a great deal for our own development as men and women. We've already looked at how our parents' behavior makes a difference in how we see God… but tonight we want to look at how images of men and women also form who we are.

The concept that there are real differences between men and women apart from pure biology may be really new and somewhat challenging to some students. It certainly runs against the cultural tide of politically correct thought. Recent scientific discoveries about gender differences are only now being published. For example, there are differences in how pharmaceuticals are absorbed into a man's body vs. a woman's. So don't be surprised if you get some quizzical looks or kids say that they just don't "get this stuff". Encourage them to let the lesson unfold and see if they're more able to grasp this concept by the end of the session.

Where do we get our images of men and women?
Desired response: Culture, magazines, newspapers, media, peers, family…etc

Are these healthy, God-reflective images of male and female?
Desired response: No, depends, stereotypes, mixed messages, all body parts…etc.

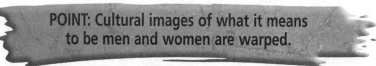

POINT: Cultural images of what it means to be men and women are warped.

If culture is not a reliable place for getting our images, let's check out a more reliable source: Scripture.

Many of the images we have in Scripture are negative but true ones—plain, everyday people like you and me with real problems. And while we don't want to imitate their behaviors, there are some healthy images we can use to see what being male and female—or having masculine and feminine characteristics—is all about.

Stage: Have students read sections of Scripture and draw answers from them regarding what characteristics their Bible people embody. Write down masculine and feminine characteristics as they are discovered.

CONTENT:

A good example of a woman with feminine characteristics is Mary.

Examine:
- Luke 1:38, 45-56 (Mary receptive to what God says, and rejoices)
- Luke 2:19 (after shepherds and angels… she ponders)

What characteristics do you see in Mary?
Desired response: Responsive, thoughtful, listens to God, receptive, eager to do what God wants, etc.

Next, check out the woman described in Proverbs 31…

Is this a quiet housewife?
Desired response: NO!

What are her actual characteristics?
Desired responses:

Admired	*Nurturing*
Makes business decisions	*Efficiently and effectively clothes her family*
Capable	*Craftsperson*
Resourceful	*Deals in expensive stuff*
Merchant	*Is given a lot of authority*
Strong	*Wise*
Good businesswoman	*Respected in the city*

(If you want more examples, check out Lydia in Acts 16:13-15 or Deborah the judge in Judges 4-5.)

Good examples of men with masculine qualities are Abraham or David.

Stage: Continue to discuss what you see in the Scriptures or what you know about Abraham and David. What are their primary characteristics? Draw out a mix of responses… List them all on overheads. Note that although David is primarily a warrior-king, he's also a responsive worship leader and a passionate, emotional guy!

Abraham: Responds to God. Leads people. Has great faith. Takes initiative.

David: Warrior. Takes initiative. Rules. Brings order (sometimes). Worship leader. Passionate (danced). Emotional (sorrowful repentance after sleeping with Bathsheba).

POINT: There are lots of admirable qualities in these prominent Bible figures. Their traits are a godly mix of what we'll call masculine and feminine characteristics.

The primary traits we see in David and Abraham are masculine. Both were men of initiative. They led, fought, and initiated according to God's design. Mary was responsive and reflective, a feminine characteristic. But both men and women are called to be responsive (we are all responsive to God). And both men and women must take action (a masculine trait). Jesus had a strong and healthy balance of the responsive and ability to take initiative. He responded to God, and acted out of that knowledge, leading relationally and with forceful and purposeful action.

We are all mixes of both, but men tend to predominate in the masculine and women tend to predominate in the feminine traits.

GENDER CONTINUUM

THE POINT: We all have both masculine and feminine characteristics. But we all need a healthy mix of both masculine and feminine traits.

TIME NEEDED: 25 Minutes

MATERIALS: Masking tape
Pink and blue paper dots or disks—approximately 4" in diameter
8-9 pink dots for each female, 8-9 blue dots for each male
2 large posterboards with feminine characteristics printed on one, and masculine characteristics printed on the other (the two lists come from the **Masculine/Feminine Differences** chart— see page 145)

PREPARATION: Prepare the "Masculine" and "Feminine" posterboards, with their respective lists of characteristics
Lay a straight line or masking tape on the floor, long enough for your group to gather around. This is your "continuum."

INTRODUCTION:

With all those characteristics, are there patterns? Types of behaviors that are typically female or typically male?

Well, there aren't inherent roles about what men and women must do, but there are some characteristics that we will label "masculine" and "feminine."

Again, we're NOT saying that all males only exhibit exclusively masculine characteristics and all females exhibit exclusively feminine ones. There's a difference between male and masculine, and between female and feminine. For example, being female means having breasts and a vagina and bearing children. Being feminine, however, means exhibiting characteristics we will call feminine. So what do we mean by feminine characteristics? Here are some general characteristics we'll define as "feminine":

- Responsive
- Free-form creative
- Caring-comfort protection
- Relational-nurturing
- Intuitive
- Being
- Holistic

Stage: List the feminine characteristics or highlight them if they've come out in discussion.

Some general characteristics we'll define as "masculine":

- Takes initiative
- Creates order
- Warrior-protection
- Task-oriented
- Rational
- "Doing"
- Compartmentalized

MASCULINE / FEMININE DIFFERENCES

	MASCULINE	**FEMININE**
Trait:	**Takes initiative/decides**	**Responsive**
Examples:	Decides cooperatively	Looks for how people feel about decision
Trait:	**Creates order**	**Free-form creative**
Examples:	Neat	Ideas from everywhere
Trait:	**Scientific**	**Artistic**
Trait:	**Warrior protection**	**Caring protection**
Examples:	Fights for what is right	Comforts and cares
Trait:	**Task-oriented more than people-oriented**	**Relational/nurturing**
Examples:	Gets job done well	Takes care of the people and their needs so task is easier
	Works with people to get job done	Gets job done so they can relate to people
Trait:	**Rational**	**Intuitive**
Examples:	Logical, orderly, scientific Decision based on facts	Ideas and gut feelings Hires based on gut feel
Trait:	**Doing**	**Being**
Examples:	Likes activity and accomplishment	Enjoys quiet and talking/listening
Trait:	**Compartmentalized**	**Holistic**

Stage: After going over and discussing characteristics, ask students to stand up or move chairs so they can see the line.

Let's stand up and make room for this long line we see on the floor.
Let's put the masculine characteristics at one end of this line, and the feminine characteristics at the other.

Stage: Put "Masculine" and "Feminine" charts at opposite ends of the continuum.

Are girls all feminine and guys all masculine?

Desired response: No.

Check out what God says in Genesis 1:26, 27: "Let us make man in our image… male and female he created them." This shows that God is actually comprised of three people who are all quite different but COMPLEMENT each other—Jesus, the Holy Spirit, and the Father! And he proceeds to make man and woman in HIS image—meaning he must have both masculine and feminine characteristics, if he creates us like that. C.S. Lewis wrote about how horrible it is to have a "man's man" or a "woman's woman"—meaning one who tries to be nothing but masculine or nothing but feminine.

> **POINT: There are masculine and feminine characteristics in all of us.**

We all have a balance of masculine and feminine. And we should. Even God does. However…

Men have God-given potential to embody the masculine characteristics—the "taking initiative" characteristics, the ordering, the rational. But no matter how sensitive or responsive a man is (and God knows men need those characteristics, too), he's still going to do those things differently than a woman. Even if a man is quite sensitive and responsive, it will be different than a woman's sensitivity and responsiveness.

Women have a God-given opportunity to be nurturing, relational, and intuitive. They have an increased capacity for those characteristics. That's certainly not to say that women can't be strong, leaders, or initiative takers. But women act in leadership differently, because they have the capacity to embody femininity.

Where else do we see this? Let's look at parents.

Who cares for and nurtures the child first?

Who ponders these things in her heart?

Who usually obsesses about the baby being okay?

Mom!

And who calls the child to walk, to risk, to try, and to have a paper route or lemonade stand?

Stage: Reference the ad on TV with kid swimming… Dad is calling him forward to jump off dock. Mom would have said no!

Where do we get these things? Mostly from our parents. And if our parents did not model these things well, then it's less likely that we'll be able to embody them well also.

Where do you fit on the continuum?

It's good to know where we fit on the masculine-feminine continuum. It also gives us a look at where we're strong and what qualities God may still want to strengthen in us. And God is pleased with where we are—he's delighted with the qualities he sees in us. Let's find out what they are…

I'm going to read some extremes and some descriptions that will help you see where you might fit into this large continuum. When you think you know where you fit, drop one of your dots there. Don't worry, everyone else is more interested in where their own dots are than in yours, so this is really anonymous.

Stage: Read masculine and feminine characteristics from the chart of differences. Use examples from situations described in chart. As you talk about one characteristic, have people drop a pink or blue dot where they think they fit. For example, for Creates Order vs. Free-form Creative, the masculine side would tend toward the scientific while the feminine side would tend toward the more artistic. Remind students that it's a continuum: "Where along this line would you put your dot?"

If there are women whose dots are on the masculine end or men whose are on the feminine end, affirm them! That's okay! Often children who had these characteristics were NOT affirmed and were ostracized or criticized. Be aware of this and point out that we all have mixtures of both.

Note also that there is often shame associated with who we are as gender people—men and women with masculine and feminine characteristics. So be extra assuring!

OPTIONAL: As a group, take the qualities listed for the biblical characters (Mary, David, Proverbs 31 wife, etc.) and drop dots for them on the continuum line. Where might these examples fit? Use this to show that godly men and women have both masculine and feminine characteristics. This is pleasing to God!

OPTIONAL: Point out if you sense participants feeling ashamed of where their dots fall. There may be guys who have strong feminine characteristics —that's good! And women with strong masculine characteristics are good, too! That is needed!

How do you feel about where the dots are? Is it surprising? Do you see trends?

Look at the line (with all the dots on it now). Are there more pink dots on one end? Are there more blue dots in one area? Discuss that—what trends do you see? (Because this is a class dealing with relationship issues, you may see more pink and blue dots at the "feminine" side of the continuum—dealing with relationships (and issues) tends to be a more feminine characteristic. That's okay, too!)

POINT: We are all a mix of masculine and feminine, false and true. But the greater capacity for the feminine is generally found in females, and the greater capacity for masculine in males.

Stage: Have students sit down if they have not already and continue teaching.

Are all these characteristics good? Do you like them?

These characteristics are POSITIVE. God loves them!

Stage: Pass out page with masculine and feminine listed (page 149) and ask students to place themselves on those lines.

POINT: God wants to bless the characteristics we do have and strengthen the ones that we have a greater capacity for and have not yet developed.

POSSIBLE SMALL GROUP QUESTIONS

SMALL GROUP GOALS:

— Talk about how we feel about our own gender.

1. What false stereotypes of your own gender have you seen?
2. Were you surprised by where you landed on the continuum?
3. What elements of the feminine or masculine are attractive to you?
4. What elements of the feminine or masculine are scary to you?
5. How does this make you feel about yourself?
6. What characteristics need to be strengthened in your life? (masculine or feminine)
7. How can we pray for you?

INDIVIDUAL CHALLENGE AS A RESULT:

— I will not despise my areas of strength, be they masculine or feminine traits.
— I will allow God to bring out in me the strength of my own gender and the good of the other.

RESOURCES AND REFERENCES

RELATED SCRIPTURES:

Genesis 1:26-27
Luke 1:38, 46-55
Luke 2:19
Proverbs 31:10-31
1 Samuel 16:18
1 Samuel 13:14
Hebrews 11:8-11, 17-19

OUTSIDE REFERENCE MATERIALS:

Andy Comiskey, *Pursuing Sexual Wholeness* (Creation House, 1989). The journey to healing for a Christian struggling with a homosexual orientation.

Leanne Payne, *The Healing Presence* (Baker, 1995). The first of two foundational books describing the identity we have from God and his healing as a result. Heavy going but excellent perspectives on psychology, theology, and philosophy.

Leanne Payne, *Restoring the Christian Soul* (Baker, 1996). The second foundational work describing the process of healing as self-acceptance, receiving forgiveness, and forgiving. (These two Leanne Payne books form the basis of much of the foundational understandings for healing involving sexual identity.)

Leanne Payne, *The Broken Image* (Baker, 1996).

Life magazine, July 1999, pages 44-57, "What's the Difference Between Boys and Girls?" by Deborah Blum.

MASCULINE/FEMININE DIFFERENCES

MASCULINE_____FEMININE

TAKES INITIATIVE/DECIDES_____RESPONSIVE

CREATES ORDER_____FREEFORM CREATIVE

WARRIOR PROTECTION_____CARING PROTECTION

TASK-ORIENTED_____RELATIONAL/NURTURING

RATIONAL_____INTUITIVE

DOING_____BEING

COMPARTMENTALIZED_____INTEGRATED

12 BI, STRAIGHT, TRANS, GAY...OR ME?

MAKING SENSE OF GENDER IDENTITY AND HOMOSEXUALITY

MAIN POINTS:

LEADER'S NOTES:

Be sure your group has gone through the Not Just Plumbing session before delving into this one!

1. How we feel about our gender has an impact on our relationships.

2. Gender identity develops in stages:

- Sense of Being—0-3 years
- Independence—3-6 years
- Gender identity—5-6 years
- Same-sex bonding—6-12 years
- Gender identity—Puberty
- Gender affirmation—Adolescence

3. Gender insecurity can result from broken parental relationships.

4. God wants to restore us to wholeness and move us beyond the stage where we may be stuck.

LESSON SEGMENTS:

The Gender-Identity Development Pyramid

Run Away or Believe It!

IN THIS LESSON...

Understand how your self-image affects your relationships...

Learn how we develop into who we are as men and women...

Find God's restoration of our self-image...

THE POINT: Our identities as men and women develop in stages. Failure to successfully get through one stage prevents complete progress, leaving us unable to move on to healthy maturity.

NEW WORDS OR CONCEPTS: Gender identity; Gender insecurity

TIME NEEDED: 30 minutes

MATERIALS: 6 cardboard boxes of increasing size
Labels for boxes: (listed largest to smallest)

Sense of Being	0-3	Mother
Independence	3-6	Father
Gender Identity	5-6	Same-sex parent
Same-sex bonding	6-12	Peers
Gender Identity	Puberty	Same-sex parent and opposite-sex parent
Gender Affirmation	Teens	Father (and peers)

INTRODUCTION:

Genesis tells us we're all created as male and female, which God called "good." As a result of Adam's sin, we became broken in our identities and unable to relate to God, to each other, or to ourselves in healthy ways. As a result, we became ashamed of our inability to manage our own lives. But instead of running to God for healing, we hid from God and were unwilling to go to him.

When we talked about gender, we saw that males have an increased capacity to exhibit masculine characteristics and females have an increased capacity to exhibit feminine characteristics.

C.S. Lewis, the author of the *Chronicles of Narnia* and *Mere Christianity* (among many others), wrote: "There ought to be a man in every woman and a woman in every man. And how horrid ones who haven't got it are; I can't bear a man's man and a woman's woman."

There's a balance of the feminine and the masculine. Some people have none of the good of the other gender to balance against the extreme opposite (for example, the stereotypical male who's all rational and doesn't have any room for emotions at all). Rather, we need to make peace with the gender that God has given us in order to get to the "good" of man and the "good" of woman in each of us and take these elements into our lives.

How do we develop good, healthy images of ourselves in terms of gender? This time, we'll look at how we develop as people of gender.

CONTENT:

Stage: As each stage of development is described, place the box on top of the previous ones.

1. SENSE OF BEING   0-3 YEARS   MOTHER

The role of mom is critical in a new baby's life. During the first few months of life and continuing for the first 2 to 3 years, a mother's love sets into us a fundamental understanding that we are wanted and loved, that we are going to be taken care of and that we matter. This sets into us a deep sense of being. It's the core from which a healthy self-esteem develops. Children who don't receive this deep sense of being loved often end up feeling like there's a hole inside that can't be filled. During this stage, infants feel like they are the center of the universe and everything revolves around them. They don't yet understand that they are separate from mom. Moms are important with their increased capacity to respond to their babies and their more relational and nurturing roles.

2. INDEPENDENCE   3-6 YEARS   FATHER

During the preschool years from toddler to around five or six, children learn they're independent from mom. This is primarily the role of the father (or significant masculine influence). It's the job of the masculine force to call children away from the protective cocoon of mom's love into exploring the world. It's Dad who encourages children to get out and try something, who encourage experimentation and taking risks, who calls children to jump to him in the water while mom is afraid that something bad will happen.

At this time, children learn they can begin to have their own lives and establish some independence. Failure to be nurtured into independence at this stage can lead to an unhealthy dependence on others and a fear of the unknown. This is actually a harder stage for boys since there is some level of tension about whether the son or the husband actually gets the mother's attention, love, and loyalty. Boys may see their fathers as competing with them for mother's love and resist separating from mom.

3. GENDER IDENTITY   5-6 YEARS   SAME-SEX PARENT

The first time children begin to understand that they are not all alike is around 5 or 6. A bonding happens at that age—little boys want to be like dad and little girls want to be like mom. There's been a lot of discussion about whether this is all cultural conditioning, but more recent studies are confirming that boys tend toward the masculine and will want to play certain roles (e.g., cowboys, soldiers, etc.) without any specific patterning or encouragement from parents. It's at this stage that we typically find children in that awkward, curious stage of wanting to know about anatomy. Playing "doctor" with other kids to see that they are different or the same as another becomes important. This kind of play isn't specifically sexual or perverted but typically is just normal curiosity. But as the culture displays sexuality more and more openly, the sexual knowledge encourages kids to understand sexual curiosity as sexual more than just inquisitive. Patterning behaviors set in as well (e.g., little boys wanting to be with dad to watch him shave or little girls wanting to play house or dress in their mom's clothes).

TESTIMONY:

Arrange for someone to offer a brief testimony about early identification.

Testimony example: Mario Bergner, author of Setting Love in Order and a former homosexual who's developed a program to help people to change from a homosexual orientation, tells of an experience with his nephew in a mall. The boy was around 5 years old and just coming to understand himself as male as opposed to female. In the middle of the mall, he blurted out "I have a penis. Uncle Mario, do you have a penis, too?" Mario answers him, "Yes, I have a penis like you and all boys and men." The awkward question out of the blue comes from the normal development process of understanding ourselves as one sex or the other.

Failure to identify oneself as "okay" as a boy or a girl may create gender insecurity, in which the child isn't able to fully accept his or her own sex and be okay with growing into the good of that gender. Many psychologists see this stage as a key to developing into a healthy heterosexuality. A lot of people dealing with homosexuality are stuck at this stage because they never get beyond the developmental task to understand who they are as male or female. And here it's the same-sex parent who is the key. A boy with no physical or emotional male presence (like when Dad is completely distant) may have a hard time understanding his maleness. Because gender confusion may develop so early in childhood, many people who struggle with homosexuality say they've been that way for their whole lives and interpret that as having been created that way. There's been lots of discussion about a "gay gene," but to date there's no scientific evidence that one exists. But even if there were a "gay gene" that would predispose one more toward the same sex, our actual behavior is still a choice that we make. Alcoholism has been shown to run in families, but taking a drink is still a choice that someone makes.

4. SAME-SEX BONDING　　　　　6-12　　　　　PEERS

Once we get into elementary school, the role of peers becomes increasingly important as we continue to differentiate ourselves from our parents. Once we've discovered that we are boys or girls, we tend to want to associate only with the same sex. This reaffirms in us our gender identity. It's at this time that we see the "boys are yucky" and "girls are gross" statements. Play tends to be more competitive between the sexes and exclusive cliques or clubs get started. This stage is also called "troop bonding." The kind of love we are learning here is "phileo"— the nonsexual love for one another.

LEADER'S NOTES:

The topic of homosexuality fascinates teens. The cultural message facing teens is that homosexuality is either genetically determined or is simply a choice based on personal preference—both positions imply that there is no moral implication. A straightforward reading of the Bible indicates that homosexual behavior runs counter to God's plan. How you address this topic, however, will be impacted by your denominational context and the position your individual church or group takes. There are many opinions about homosexual behavior throughout the Christian spectrum, but I believe there are some underlying principles that are biblical and that would find general agreement among most Christians

1. Homosexual behavior is not a different category of sin. The church has often branded homosexual behavior (and sexual sin in general) as a worse evil than other sins. But all sin separates us from God, whether it's homosexual behavior, heterosexual addiction, pride, gluttony, or self-righteousness.

2. Homophobia—the fear of homosexuals —has no place at all in the church or in your group. An all-too-common response to the more extreme statements from the homosexual community is to declare homosexuals as degenerate, perverted, or depraved. Often this is done in derision and with labeling ("perverts", "queers", etc.), not in love. Extreme forms of homophobia often spring from a fear that homosexuality is like some communicable disease that others can catch. But you may have kids who don't understand their own ambivalent feelings. When homosexuality is polarized to extremes, kids who're struggling can only stay hidden in shame or completely walk away from the church or youth group. Either response isolates them from God, who wants them in relationship and healing.

3. As Christians we are called to sexual purity—that means sex only within marriage and celibacy outside of marriage. Whether our orientation is gay or straight, acting out sexually outside of marriage is sinful.

4. Homosexual action is different than homosexual feelings. We all struggle with temptations. Jesus himself was tempted "in every way that we are" but without sin. (Hebrews 4: 15) It's likely that Jesus faced sexual temptation, too. Just being tempted isn't wrong! Kids who struggle with homosexual feelings often feel dirty or unworthy of God's love. Realizing that can free struggling teens and encourage them to look for the way out that God provides.

5. God can change anything in our lives. We are new creatures in Christ and no longer slaves to sin. (Romans 6:17-18) The homosexual community maintains that sexual orientation cannot be changed. There are thousands of cases where this has been proven wrong. And there's a reluctant but growing acceptance in the psychological community that sexual orientation is not fixed for all time. For those who want to change a homosexual orientation, there are resources. Exodus International is an umbrella organization of hundreds of Christian "ex-gay" ministries that can help. For more information check out www.exodusinternational.org. Kids who're struggling desperately to change need hope and encouragement—not condemnation, isolation, or doubt that change is possible.

5. GENDER IDENTITY   PUBERTY   SAME-SEX PARENT AND OPPOSITE-SEX PARENT

When we hit puberty, hormones kick in and everything becomes sexualized as we develop into our adult sexuality. We move from the same-sex grouping to finding the other sex "strangely attractive." We all have seen movies about that moment when the boy goes from "Girls? Yuck!" to being attracted to them in a heartbeat. At this stage, our gender identities need reaffirming by both the same-sex and the opposite-sex parent. Girls begin needing to know their fathers affirm their womanhood and that she is attractive. A bouquet from Dad can be meaningful for a lifetime. She finds that when her dad treats her well, she should expect to be treated well by others, also. Boys, too, need to know that their mothers bless and affirm their manhood. Puberty also brings that gawky growth spurt when we get all arms and legs and become uncoordinated. Parents need to affirm their kids that they are still okay and still good even when there's so much change going on.

6. GENDER AFFIRMATION   TEENS   FATHER (AND PEERS)

As adolescence proceeds, the role of parents in the child's life declines and the peer group predominates. Gender identity is either reaffirmed by peers of either sex or can be damaged by the taunting criticism that makes junior high and early high school such awful times for many kids. It's at this time that "eros" love is learned, when the quality of love involves sexual and romantic feelings. Dad's ability to encourage and affirm is key here in building confidence in the teenager.

WRAP-UP:

POINT: Development of gender identity has multiple stages. We can't progress fully to later stages if earlier ones are still incomplete.

What would happen to a girl if she gets stuck and never really accomplishes the independence stage?

Desired Response: Have the group fill in what might happen to the girl. Possible responses are that she's constantly fearful and terribly clingy. She's afraid to date and very insecure about herself.

Stage: Continue asking questions that the group can speculate on regarding the impact of not fully getting through a period of development.

Where there's an interruption in the development of our understanding of our-selves as people with a sex and a gender orientation, we can get stuck. While we obviously continue to grow up physically, our emotional maturity may be stunted since we cannot completely appropriate all of what we need to accom-plish during later stages. When you get stuck, it's important to pray for God's healing for that stage. Sometimes it takes a while to understand some of the deeper and earlier hurts first. Healing prayer is a tool that God uses often to meet the earlier unmet developmental needs.

Gender insecurity means not knowing how you feel about yourself as a male or as a female. Do you embrace and enjoy your maleness and your femaleness? Or do you sometimes wish you weren't a boy or a girl?

Gender insecurity WILL express itself relationally. For some, this will man-ifest itself by running to relationships with the same gender in order to make up for their own perceived lack—or by running away from the same sex in reaction against their gender, especially the false expressions of gender.

Homosexual relationships are an example: In some children, the lack of gender security can cause fixations toward members of the same sex in an attempt to get the gender identity they were denied. At puberty, this all gets sexualized and often works its way out via homosexual relationships. But it's much broader than that, as all manner of skewed patterns and attitudes come from gender insecurity. An abusive father can lead to a passive, emasculated male, afraid to take leadership or authority. An abusive father can also lead to an angry male who wants to use his sexuality to dominate women.

But God wants to restore you to make up for things that are lacking. (Joel 2:25) Take a look at yourself and see if there are places or stages you weren't able to complete. Where do your boxes fit and where do they need to be restored?

RUN AWAY OR BELIEVE IT!

THE POINT: There are typical patterns regarding how we detach from bad role models and make vows to not be like them—or internalize our mistreatment and feel self-hatred.

TIME NEEDED: 20 minutes

MATERIALS: Copies of role-plays (page 158)

PREPARATION: Copy the role-plays and cut slips for students

INTRODUCTION:

POINT: Broken relationships with same-sex parents can block development of gender identity.

When we are mistreated we tend to do one of two things: Either we run away from the mistreatment and wall ourselves off…or we take the mistreatment inside and figure that we must have somehow deserved it.

This may not have been outward and tangible abuse; it depends on the sensitivity of the child. The key issue is whether the parent is a worthy role model. We react to our parents in a couple of ways:

1. RUN AWAY.

Some kids wall themselves off from abusive parents to avoid being hurt or to not be like them. This breakdown leaves a hole. If we need our parents to help solidify our gender identity but we cut them off, then we are missing out a part of the blessing that we need from our parents. Our legitimate need for true and healthy same-sex identification, nurture, and love may result in our inability to take on the characteristics of the same-sex parent. When this begins to happen, the parents themselves become the symbol of something that gets much bigger than the specific situation. The person may tend to generalize to all members of that sex or see every problem they have as stemming from the source of the broken relationship with mom or dad.

2. BELIEVE IT.

The other response to mistreatment is to agree with it and welcome it. We take the abuse inside and assume that since our parents are the authority, they must be right—and assume we're the bad ones! This can lead to rejection of the child as a genderized person and lead to confusion, fear, and insecurity.

CONTENT:

We're going to role-play some typical interactions between parents and children to illustrate either "run away" (vow never to be like them) or "believe it."

Stage: Have group split into pairs or threes. Distribute one role-play suggestion slip to each group. Give each group 5 minutes to come up with a 1-minute sketch to illustrate the situation, but the role-play must end with the line given. Introduce each group and allow each to play their piece. At the end of each sketch, have the rest identify what was going on.

WRAP-UP:

> **POINT: God wants to restore us to wholeness and set us free.**

How have you responded when your parents haven't been there in all the ways you needed them? If we've reacted with walls and vows to not be like them, God can deal with this. He can free us from those vows so that we can receive the good of the masculine or the feminine—even from broken people. (We're all broken people, remember!) If we've reacted by agreeing with the mistreatment and letting it inside us, God wants to free us from our self-hatred. He wants to free us so we can know we're worthwhile to him. God wants meet our unmet needs and let us mature whole and healthy, relating to others as they really are—and as we really are!

POSSIBLE SMALL GROUP QUESTIONS

SMALL GROUP GOALS:

- Understand what foundation blocks are missing in participants' lives.
- Understand where patterns of relating come from.

1. Where were you in the pyramid—what blocks did you lack or need work on?
2. What kind of a role model is your mother? Your father?
3. Is your parents' relationship a good model for you and for the type of relationship you would like to have?
4. How has your father affected how you feel about yourself as a man or woman?
5. How has your mother affected how you feel about yourself as a man or woman?
6. Did you wall yourself off from either your mom or dad in order to keep from being hurt?
7. How did your opposite sex parent help you to "make peace" with the opposite sex?
8. Do your friends build you up with regard to your gender identity or tear you down?

INDIVIDUAL CHALLENGE:

- I will treat all people—gay or straight—as Christ would treat them.
- I will behave with respect to the new identity God has for me rather than my own, imperfect self-image.
- If I'm stuck at a development stage, I will seek God's help to get unstuck.

RESOURCES AND REFERENCES

RELATED SCRIPTURES:

Genesis (the creation story)
Hebrews 4:15

OUTSIDE REFERENCE MATERIALS:

Mario Bergner, *Setting Love in Order* (Baker, 1995). The accounts of Mario's road to healing from homosexuality can be very helpful for those struggling or for those who desire to understand more about homosexual orientation.

Andy Comiskey, *Pursuing Sexual Wholeness* (Creation House, 1989). The journey to healing for a Christian struggling with homosexuality.

Elizabeth Moberly, *Homosexuality: Toward a New Christian Ethic* (James Clark and Co., 1983) Out of print now but a foundational understanding of the development of gender identity and gender confusion. Keen insights into the role of the same-sex parent in gender identity development.

Leanne Payne, *The Healing Presence* (Baker, 1995). The first of two foundational books describing the identity we have from God and his healing as a result. Heavy going but excellent perspectives on psychology, theology, and philosophy.

Leanne Payne, *Restoring the Christian Soul* (Baker, 1996). The second foundational work describing the process of healing as self-acceptance, receiving forgiveness, and forgiving. These two Leanne Payne works form the basis of much of the foundational understandings for healing involving sexual identity for this curriculum.

RUN AWAY OR BELIEVE IT!
IMPROVISATION ROLE PLAYS

1. RUN AWAY

Dad is angry and critical. Mom is wimpy and kind of flaky. They have a fight about how she spends money. Child looks on and tries to defend Mom. This doesn't work very well.

Sketch ends: "I'll never be like that when I grow up."

---

2. RUN AWAY

Mom is overprotective and afraid that her high school son/daughter will get in trouble at a party over the weekend. Dad is very permissive and says it's okay to go—just don't get into too much trouble. The discussion gets a bit extreme.

Sketch ends: "That's not what I want to be like—ever!"

---

3. RUN AWAY

Dad is a social misfit, making inappropriate and obnoxious comments to everyone. Mom is a gossip and can't keep anything quiet. They are at a restaurant with the son/daughter. They start to do their thing and get into a pretty extreme situation. The son/daughter tries without success to calm things down but ends up absolutely embarrassed by them.

Sketch ends: "I don't ever want to be like that."

---

4. BELIEVE IT (needs a female to play the daughter)

Dad treats all women as sex objects and makes rude and crass remarks all the time. The daughter sees Dad making fun of Mom and others and starts to get the same treatment. Dad gets condescending and coaches daughter about how to treat guys. Daughter starts to feel like that when its time for her to date, that's what she can expect from guys.

Sketch ends: "I guess that's just what I should expect to get."

---

5. BELIEVE IT

Mom is demanding and constantly needing to be taken care of. Dad is a wimp and also needs to be taken care of. Mom starts to get son/daughter to take care of her as well. Everything in the family revolves around helping out mom's inability to do anything. Son/daughter starts to feel like his/her only reason for existence is to meet mom's needs.

Sketch ends: "Is that what I'm made for?"